Ancient Peoples and Places

EAST
ANGLIA

General Editor

DR GLYN DANIEL

Ancient Peoples and Places

EAST ANGLIA

R. Rainbird Clarke

60 PHOTOGRAPHS
30 LINE DRAWINGS
5 CHARTS
AND 13 MAPS

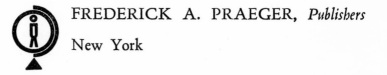

FREDERICK A. PRAEGER, *Publishers*

New York

THIS IS VOLUME FOURTEEN IN THE SERIES
Ancient Peoples and Places
GENERAL EDITOR: DR GLYN DANIEL

BOOKS THAT MATTER
Published in the United States of America
in 1960 by Frederick A. Praeger, Inc., Publishers
64 University Place, New York 3, N.Y.
All rights reserved
© Thames and Hudson, London, 1960
Library of Congress catalog card number 60-7377
Printed in Great Britain by Jarrold and Sons, Ltd., Norwich

CONTENTS

CONTENTS

6

ILLUSTRATIONS

7

8

Foreword

THE SCALE of this book precludes notes referring to the detailed evidence on which the author's conclusions are based, but the select bibliography indicates some of the more important work already published. The absence of detailed documentation does not imply that the author is unaware of the immense debt he owes to his archaeological predecessors in East Anglia since the sixteenth century. Most of these are beyond the range of his thanks, but to his contemporaries, especially colleagues in the Norfolk Research Committee and archaeologists working for the Ancient Monuments Inspectorate of the Ministry of Works, he wishes to express his deep gratitude for information on unpublished investigations and new interpretations of the older evidence. For liberal help in assembling the relevant material from Suffolk he desires to record his thanks to the Curator of the Ipswich Museums, and from those portions of adjacent counties covered by the distribution maps, to the Archaeology Officer of the Ordnance Survey. It should be made abundantly clear, however, that the author alone is responsible for the marshalling of this mass of data and for the unorthodox conclusions he has sometimes ventured to draw from it.

The writing of this book would have been even more difficult but for the unremitting help in all stages of its production given by his museum colleague, Miss Barbara Green, and the author is deeply grateful for her collaboration over the last two years. He also thanks his friends, Mr Charles Green, Mr C. H. Lewton-Brain and Dr O. K. Schram, who have scrutinized much of the text, eliminated errors of fact and modified some of his more outrageous suggestions. To other friends, too numerous to be mentioned individually, he is grateful for advice on various points and takes this opportunity of recording his gratitude. Finally, the author thanks his publishers for their patience and co-operation. If this book achieves any success, this will be indicated by the speed with which it stimulates others to supersede its conclusions.

R. R. C.

CHAPTER I

The Setting

E AST ANGLIA—the counties of Norfolk and Suffolk—lies on the eastern seaboard of England and looks out across the narrow seas to the continent, with which it is more intimately linked than with the rest of Britain. Because of the geological structure and physical configuration of the region, spectacular monuments like stone circles and hilltop fortresses, so conspicuous in other regions, are absent. Nevertheless, with few exceptions, the evidence for human activity in East Anglia in every period is abundant, and it offers a more continuous history than do most parts of Britain. The story to be outlined in the ensuing chapters can clearly lay no claim to finality: some statements will doubtless be disproved by fresh discoveries made between its date of composition and publication. The casual finds and deliberate investigations of the last decade have shed such a flood of light that one may safely predict that many modifications to the facts and their interpretation will follow in the next few years. In any event all reconstructions of the past by archaeological methods are necessarily incomplete and dis-torted. This book must therefore be regarded as an interim report summarizing the present position in an investigation which will never be complete.

East Anglia forms part of the English Lowland and, as a seventeenth-century writer, Robert Reyce, said, 'is void of any great hills, high mountains, or steep rocks; notwithstanding the which it is not always so low, or flat, but that in every place it is severed and divided with little hills easy for ascent and pleasant rivers watering the low valleys.' Much of East Anglia lies below the 200-foot contour and so earns the epithet of 'low-lying' given to it by those accustomed to more hilly regions. At only a few points in south-west Suffolk does the surface rise above

Fig. 1   East Anglia—Sub-regions

the 400/foot contour; in Norfolk it is rare to find any land over 300 feet, while parts of Fenland lie below mean sea/ level.

The geographical region of East Anglia is a wider area than that covered by this book. The administrative boundaries of Norfolk and Suffolk tend to follow rivers, thus arbitrarily dividing these counties from the rest of this distinctive region. The two counties form a rough square with curving sides, each some seventy miles long. Few places in it are more than thirty miles from the sea/coast or an estuary, and this emphasizes that Norfolk and Suffolk with their long coastline from the Wash to Felixstowe are maritime counties.

The main groups of rivers which drain the region are shown on the map. The watershed between the East Coast rivers and the Wash rivers lies in an area of heavy soil, chiefly derived from boulder clay. This wide tract of boulder clay runs down the centre of the two counties and is continuous except where it is dissected by river valleys. It formerly supported thick woodland which impeded communications between the more habitable areas to its east and west. Another physiographical feature common to both counties is the ridge of chalkland, between five and ten miles wide, forming a belt of relatively open country on the western side of the central clay area. This corridor connects southern England with East Anglia, and, passing through Cambridgeshire, runs through north/west Suffolk and west Norfolk to reach the coast at Hunstanton.

The region of East Anglia can be divided into three main zones—a central clay belt and two areas of lighter soils—and these can be further sub/divided on the basis of their varying soils and vegetation. Some of these sub/regions were more attractive than others to early farmers, because they possessed soils supporting a light growth of woodland which could be effectively cleared with primitive equipment, and some descrip/ tion of these distinctive areas is therefore needed:

Fig. 1

The Fenland—This stretches from the edge of the upland in west Norfolk and north-west Suffolk into Lincolnshire and Cambridgeshire. The whole area is low-lying, with silt chiefly in the north near the Wash and peat in the south, from which rise a few islands of older and harder material.

The Greensand Belt—The northern portion of this sub-region lies on the west Norfolk ridge and extends from Snettisham in the north to the neighbourhood of Downham Market. Its name indicates the sandy nature of the soil, today mainly supporting heathland and birch woods, but there are patches of clay which would formerly have been more densely wooded.

The Good Sand Region—This was so named by Arthur Young, the eighteenth-century agriculturalist, but only deserved the name after the agricultural improvements of the seventeenth and eighteenth centuries. This upland area lies between the Greensand Belt and the north Norfolk coast and reaches as far east as Cromer. Its soils are variable; some are chalky, some sands and gravels with medium and light loams which formerly supported wide tracts of heath. Its coastal fringe, with salt marshes and sand dunes separating the upland from the coast-line, is sometimes considered a separate area.

Mid-Norfolk—The extensive cover of boulder clay in this up-land area gives rise to strong loams which were once thickly wooded and even now support extensive oak woods and abundant hedgerow timber. The eastern side of the area is dissected by wide deep valleys.

The Loam Region—This region stretches from Norwich north-wards to the Cromer-Holt ridge and to the coast from Cromer to Palling. The area is low-lying and scenically unexciting except on the beaches, overshadowed by clay cliffs up to 200 feet high. Glacial loams predominate, as its name indicates, and there was formerly much woodland, though not as dense as in South and Mid-Norfolk. On the whole its soils are light to medium, and there are considerable stretches of sand and gravels, many of which supported heathland though much of this is now under plough.

Broadland—Lying between the Loam Region, South Norfolk and the sea, Broadland includes both an alluvial area and upland. The alluvial area lies in the river valleys where a wide expanse of grazing marsh covers the silt of the former 'Great Estuary'. The upland consists of the Norwich-Reedham-Acle peninsula and the island of Flegg with their extremely fertile soils, and the peninsula of Lothingland between Yarmouth and Lowestoft with its sands and gravels forming a less fertile soil which supports little woodland.

South Norfolk—It is not easy to draw a frontier between this area and Mid-Norfolk, but its soils on the whole are heavier and were formerly covered with thick woodland, while its elevation is generally less than in the central part of the county.

Breckland—This sub-region occupies a wide area of south-west Norfolk and north-west Suffolk and owes its distinctive character to a layer of sand overlying chalk and boulder clay. Until its recent afforestation, this low plateau has been mainly heathland for many centuries.

Plate 1

Chalk Downland—Only a small area of Suffolk around Newmarket comes within this sub-region, which extends south-westward across Cambridgeshire, and it provides a belt of relatively open country between Fenland and Breckland on the north and the wooded clay country on the south.

High Suffolk—This area is largely boulder clay forming a continuation of that of South Norfolk but the soils are on the whole heavier, particularly towards the south-west where the surface rises to over 400 feet. This sub-region was formerly densely forested and is still well wooded.

Date	Climatic Phases	Geology	Forest	Periods
2000				Modern
1500		Minor rise in sea-level	Alder	
			Oak	Medieval
1000			Elm	Late Saxon
		Fall in sea-level	Birch	Early Saxon
500	Sub-Atlantic			
A.D.	(cold and wet)	Minor rise		Roman
B.C.		in sea-level (Fen silt)		Iron Age
500				
		Fall in sea-level (Upper Peat in Fens)		Bronze Age
1000				
	Sub-Boreal			
1500	(mild)	Rise in sea-level (Fen clay)		
2000			Alder	Neolithic
2500			Oak	
			Elm	
3000			Lime	
	Atlantic (warm and wet)			
4000				
		Fall in sea-level (Lower Peat in Fens)		
5000				Mesolithic
			Pine Hazel	
	Boreal (warm and dry)			
6000				
		Rapid rise in sea-level	Pine	
7000				
	Pre-Boreal (less cold)	Floor of southern North Sea dry	Pine Birch	
8000				
	Late-Glacial (cold)		Birch copses	Upper Palaeolithic

Chart A *Post-Glacial Periods and Environment*

The Sandlings—This stretches along the Suffolk coast from the Stour estuary to Lowestoft. Its moderately fertile soils consist of glacial sands and gravels, and the sandy loams of the Crag. Today much of the area is open heathland and this was still more extensive in the past.

Plate 2

It will be apparent by now that the region of East Anglia is anything but homogeneous, and the picture becomes even more complex when it is realized that the setting has not remained static during the last ten thousand years. It has been modified on the one hand by the operation of certain natural forces and on the other by human activities. The principal natural factors affecting the appearance of the East Anglian landscape in the past have been changes of climate, controlling vegetation, and vertical movements of land and sea, enlarging or restricting the areas available for human settlement.

The sequence of climatic changes in the Palaeolithic Age will be discussed in the next chapter. Here we shall begin at about 8000 B.C., at the conventional boundary between the Upper Palaeolithic and Mesolithic cultures. At this time the last cold period of the Late-Glacial phase, associated with tundra conditions and birch copses, gave place rapidly to a milder climate. The evidence for the type of vegetation in this, as in succeeding phases, comes largely from the identification of pollen grains of trees and plants recovered from the peats and muds of bogs and lakes. In East Anglia most of it derives from borings made in Fenland, in the Breckland meres, on the north Norfolk coast and in the valleys of Broadland.

The milder climate of the Pre-Boreal phase, with its closed birch forests, evolved soon after 7000 B.C. into the warmer and drier climate of the Boreal phase. This climatic change was responsible for a wide expansion of pine and hazel, though the dominant pine and birch woods were displaced before the end of the phase, about 5000 B.C., by the onset of mixed-oak forest, chiefly oak and elm with some lime and alder. During the latter part of the Boreal phase and the ensuing Atlantic phase, the climate attained an optimum when the mean temperatures were higher by about 2·5 degrees Centigrade than those prevailing today. At the beginning of the Atlantic phase the climate became pronouncedly more oceanic, and this increasing wetness stimulated the development of deciduous forest. There does not seem to be much evidence that the optimum conditions of the Atlantic phase continued into the Sub-Boreal, which was probably cooler and drier. Oak and alder remained dominant throughout the Sub-Boreal phase, which lasted from about 2500 to 500 B.C. The Sub-Atlantic phase, which succeeded the Sub-Boreal, started with a rapid climatic deterioration, reverting to moister conditions with lower summer temperatures and less severe winters. With this colder and wetter climate, the lime tree almost disappeared from the Fenland margins, while the birch and beech became more abundant. In Fenland woods gave way to wet expanses of sedge or shallow water.

The second major factor modifying the East Anglian land-scape since the Last Glaciation has been the vertical move-ment of the land in relation to the sea. In glacial times, water had been abstracted from the seas to form ice-sheets and had caused a maximum fall of sea-level of perhaps 200 feet. With the gradual melting of ice during the warmer conditions of post-glacial times this water was restored to the sea and its level rose correspondingly. In addition to these fluctuations of sea-level, there have been associated movements of the land. During the glacial periods in northern Europe the weight of ice, in places many thousands of feet thick, depressed the underlying rocks. When the ice sheets melted, the removal of this burden allowed the land to rise slowly but not evenly. This ill-balanced recovery, with spasmodic elevation and depression, continues to the present time.

Until about 6000 B.C., East Anglia was still united to the

continent with the southern half of the North Sea dry and, at the beginning of the Boreal phase, a coastline stretching from the present coast of Yorkshire round the Dogger Bank to join the western shore of Jutland. The rise of sea-level during this period created the North Sea as we know it, by flooding over a low-lying plain traversed by the lower reaches of the Rhine, the Thames and other rivers, and these new maritime conditions may have accelerated the transition to the Atlantic climate. By the end of the period the sea had risen to within 70 feet of its present relative level, and the waters continued to rise, though less rapidly, throughout the Atlantic phase.

At several points on the Norfolk coast, and especially off Thornham and Titchwell, the trunks and stools of ancient trees can be seen at very low tides. Analysis of the pollen in the peat with which these trees are associated suggests that they were growing in the Atlantic phase, and the finding at Thornham of a polished flint axehead embedded in a tree trunk and of other tools elsewhere, shows that this area was dry land and still habitable during Neolithic times. This is confirmed by the discovery of Neolithic pottery in the Lower Peat of the Fens at Peacock's Farm, Shippea Hill, Cambridgeshire, at 15 feet below modern sea-level. This site would clearly have been uninhabitable unless the water-level was then lower. A century or so after 2000 B.C., towards the end of Neolithic times, extensive flooding took place and the sea rose to a few feet above its present level. This led to the submergence of a large area off the north-west coast of Norfolk, to the deposition of a semi-marine Buttery Clay in the Fens and possibly, though this is not certain, to the deposition of clay deep in the valleys of Broadland. The brackish lagoon which at this period covered much of Fenland was again replaced by freshwater fen as the result of a slight fall in sea-level, and the Upper Peat then formed throughout the Fenland basin and in other low-lying areas. This took place during the Bronze Age.

The worsening of the climate about 500 B.C. has already been noted. These colder, wetter conditions of the Sub-Atlantic may have been partly responsible for the formation of large shallow meres in Fenland, which was largely uninhabitable during the Iron Age when this climatic deterioration was supplemented by a widespread submergence. In Broadland it led to a deposit of silt up the eastern valleys, with open estuarine conditions stretching far inland and fen and swamp in the upper reaches of the rivers.

Until recently it was thought that further submergence had taken place continuously since Roman times, but from fresh evidence obtained in preparing foundations for the South Denes power station at Great Yarmouth, and elsewhere, it seems likely that by Late Saxon times the land had again emerged, and until the late thirteenth century stood at least ten feet higher in relation to the sea than it does now. A rapid re-submergence in the late thirteenth and fourteenth centuries led in Broadland and Fen-land to the embanking of the rivers and the cutting of drainage dykes to prevent the flooding of the adjacent marshes. This rise in water-level also led to the abandonment of the deep peat cuttings now known as Broads. The full extent of our loss of archaeological material by coastal erosion, due in part to changing land and sea levels, will never be known.

The natural changes in the East Anglian environment have been of vital importance in controlling the distribution of population, but eventually Man was able, to some extent, to modify the landscape to meet his economic needs. Man's greatest achievement has undoubtedly been the destruction of the natural woodlands, but human activity during the periods covered by this book has also left its distinctive imprint in the construction of canals and sea defences, in the excavation of deep pits, in the conversion of virgin land into arable and in the erection of towns, villages and farms.

Although wood was used in Palaeolithic and Mesolithic

times for making tools and constructing shelters, these inroads on the woodlands were on such a small scale that natural regeneration soon healed the scars. The deforestation of Neo-lithic times, undertaken in the interests of farming, was the first large-scale attempt by Man to modify his environment. Further encroachments on the forests took place during the Roman Age, but the great period of deforestation was during the Late Saxon Age, when the land hunger of an increasing population caused the wholesale destruction of woodland and its conversion to villages and arable.

The twin problems of flooding and communications are always present for the inhabitants of low-lying areas, and artificial waterways have been dug in an attempt to solve them. This is conspicuously so in Fenland where almost all the water-ways now in use are of human origin. Most of these have been made since the mid-seventeenth century but some are as old as the Roman Age. At this period the main natural drainage of the Fens flowed past the future site of Wisbech through the channel later known as The Wellstream, of which the Lark, Little Ouse and Wissey were tributaries. The present lower course of the Great Ouse then only existed as far south as Stowbridge. This system survived throughout the Anglo-Saxon period into the Early Middle Ages. Before the end of the thirteenth century the outlet of The Wellstream at Wisbech became choked, and the waters of the Little Ouse and Wissey were diverted into an artificial channel linked to the Great Ouse, and so running into the sea at King's Lynn.

Closely linked with the drainage and occupation of Fenland is the question of artificial defences against the ever-present threat of sea flooding. It is possible that Roman defences against the sea existed, but they have never been identified. The 'Sea-Bank', which runs for 150 miles round the margin of the Wash and has been calculated to contain over ten million tons of material, is traditionally attributed to the Romans, but there is little evidence to support this. Documents show that this embankment was in existence by 1178 when it was breached, and recent fieldwork has shown that it was raised in height on several occasions, presumably in response to rising water-levels. It has been claimed by place-name specialists that the names of Wal-soken, Wal-ton and Wal-pole, recorded as early as the tenth century, imply that the 'Sea-Bank' was in existence at the time these villages were named.

Some of the most impressive examples in East Anglia of human activity can be seen in Broadland. Until recently the extensive and delightful tracts of water known as Broads were considered natural formations, but the combined evidence of stratigraphy, medieval documents and archaeological dis-coveries has shown conclusively that they are merely vast flooded pits, dug to extract peat for fuel. The beginning of this industry cannot be dated exactly, but it probably started before the Norman Conquest, perhaps as early as the late ninth century. It flourished in Early Medieval times, coming to an end in the fourteenth and fifteenth centuries when a rising water-level flooded the workings.

In later chapters the human occupation of East Anglia will be discussed in detail but a few generalizations may not be out of place here. From Neolithic until Early Saxon times, two main areas of settlement, separated by forest, may be distin-guished, the Breckland Zone and the Ipswich Zone. The Breckland Zone includes west Norfolk and north-west Suffolk —an area drained by rivers flowing through Fenland into the Wash. The Ipswich Zone may be defined as that portion of Suffolk which lay east of the central forest belt. Both these zones owe their dense occupation in most post-glacial periods to their easily tilled soil and relatively open terrain; where wood-land formerly existed, as in Breckland, it was easily cleared. It was only in Late Saxon and Medieval times that the heavier soils of South and Mid-Norfolk and of High Suffolk were extensively cultivated, owing to the demand of an expanding population for new farmland.

Waterways are the obvious routes into the interior for invaders and traders arriving from the continent, and were clearly used in almost every period. It was, of course, not only the Fenland rivers and the estuaries of the Ipswich Zone which were used by sea-borne travellers; to a lesser extent, advantage was at some time taken of the estuaries of the Bure, Waveney and Yare near Yarmouth, and of the smaller havens all round the coast by boat-loads of immigrants from across the North Sea. These harbours were also important as centres for local trade, as coastal naviga-tion along the East Anglian shore was often quicker and cheaper than the overland route through thickly forested country.

Despite the density of the woodlands in central Norfolk and Suffolk, it should not be assumed that east-west communications were impossible. They were obviously essential for contact between the Breckland and Ipswich Zones, and maps showing the distribution of archaeological finds indicate that corridors existed through the forest belt during most periods. Three of these corridors can be recognized—from the headwaters of the Wensum to those of the Nar in west Norfolk; across the narrow watershed between the sources of the Waveney and Little Ouse on the Norfolk-Suffolk boundary; and from the Gipping valley to the Lark valley.

Another land route of great importance lay along the chalk ridge of north-west Suffolk and west Norfolk, where the country was relatively open and the going easy. The course of most ancient trackways was somewhat flexible, and to label any particular modern road as an ancient highway is a rather dubious procedure. However, the series of roads generically known as the Icknield Way indicate approximately this main route from the Thames to Hunstanton, thus linking Wessex with East Anglia. Hunstanton was not the northern terminus of this route, for the presence of prehistoric trackways and

Roman roads continuing on the Lincolnshire Wolds strongly suggest that some ferry service across the mouth of the Wash, then narrower than it is at present, linked Norfolk with Lincolnshire. Many lesser trackways certainly existed in the more densely populated areas of East Anglia, as may be inferred from the distribution of various types of monuments and small finds, but their courses cannot be plotted precisely.

From the evidence of air-photographs, East Anglia has clearly suffered the loss of many monuments of all periods, whether constructed of flint, stone, brick, chalk, clay, gravel, sand, turf or timber. This widespread destruction is due to several causes. The natural decay of timber has caused the collapse of all structures of which it formed the basic framework, while the submergence of low-lying land in Fenland and Broadland has led to the deposition of clays and peats over surfaces which had once been inhabited. The lack of first-class building material in the region has led people of succeeding periods to demolish earlier buildings. The land hunger of Early Medieval times led to the removal of obstacles to agriculture, while the same process was followed on an even larger scale in the eighteenth and nineteenth centuries when the acreage under plough was increased by cultivating waste lands. In the twentieth century, the use of mechanical power and heavier machinery has led to the widespread practice of deep ploughing and so to the rapid and final obliteration of many of those earthworks which still survived. Nevertheless, the past still lives on in the present and the activities of our forebears influence our own activities. The nuclei of our present villages and towns date back to at least Late Saxon times and beneath some of our fields the outlines of Roman and Medieval cultivation can still be detected. Traffic congestion is frequently the result of the siting of a castle, monastery or bridge of the eleventh century, while the credit for many of our better roads is primarily due to Roman military engineers. In places the skyline is still broken by the gentle swell of Bronze Age burial mounds and the ramparts and ditches of Iron Age forts, while the tremendous earthworks of Norman castles still dominate their immediate surroundings. Our streets and lanes are even now peopled by individuals whose physical characteristics betray a biological connexion with one or more of the numerous invaders whose fortunes we shall chronicle, and when East Anglian countrymen open their mouths, their choice of words and intonation reveal something of the cultural history of their ancestors. Even the rapid communications of the twentieth century have not completely welded East Anglia into a cultural and economic unity. Yet the province has a distinct pride in its varied ancestry, in its hospitable assimilation of wave after wave of immigrants, and still boasts an independent outlook, undeterred by the judgments of the Metropolis.

CHAPTER II

The Palaeolithic

M AN'S FIRST APPEARANCE in East Anglia was probably between 400,000 and 500,000 years ago, in the period known as the Palaeolithic or Old Stone Age, which lasted until about 8000 B.C. During this immense period, fifty times as long as the whole of the rest of human history, East Anglia was in the intermittent grip of an ice age. On four occasions glaciers invaded East Anglia from the west or north and then gradually melted and retreated. The intervals between the major ice advances lasted several thousand years and are known as interglacial periods, while lesser retreats of the ice also took place during the actual glaciations themselves. When the ice melted, great spreads of clay, sand and gravel were left behind, which were often disturbed by later ice advances, or by alternating freeze and thaw outside the area sealed by ice. The ice sheets were responsible not only for the creation of many surface soils, but also for moulding the configuration of East Anglia. The formation of glaciers led to a considerable lowering of sea-level, thus linking Britain with the continent, from which it was again separated when water was returned to the sea through the melting of the ice.

It would be a mistake to think of Palaeolithic man as being in intimate contact with the ice; most hunters of this period probably never saw an ice-sheet at any time in their lives, for their existence in East Anglia was restricted to the interglacial periods, when glaciers had retreated to the north. Evidence for the appearance of the East Anglian countryside during the interglacial periods has been obtained from a few deposits which were not destroyed by the subsequent movements of ice. Bones and teeth of the larger animals that roamed this area are plentiful but have often been moved by water from the locality in which the beast died or was drowned. Similarly, flint tools made by the local population during the Palaeolithic have been transported by water or ice from the spot at which they were discarded and are found, often battered, in clay, sand or gravel beds. These flint tools are the only archaeological material of this period as yet discovered in East Anglia, though at Clacton in north Essex the tip of a wooden spear has survived.

Man's earliest tools were probably naturally fractured flints with sharp edges, but it is obviously impossible to distinguish these from other natural flints which have not been utilized. The first stage in tool-making would probably be for a hunter to select a flint of suitable shape, and improve it by striking off small flakes round the edges. These again must, of necessity, be difficult to recognize. A further stage of advance may be claimed when the flint object bears not only the scars of random flaking, but the marks of purposive blows from two or three directions only, made to a definite design which can be easily distinguished. Such, it has been claimed, are some of the flints that have been recovered from the Suffolk Bone Bed and the Norfolk Stone Bed. These alleged tools are often known as eoliths or 'dawn stones', and the appearance of some is strongly suggestive of intelligent design especially when seen in the isolation of a museum; but they are less convincing when viewed in company with the other flints composing these deposits, which range from the obviously natural to the apparently artificial. Theoretically, there is no reason why Man should not have existed in East Anglia at this time, as undoubted tools of an earlier date have been found in other parts of the world. There are, however, grave objections to accepting these Sub-Crag industries (so-called because the Bone and Stone Beds lie beneath Crags of shelly sandstones) as definite proof that Man was living here and flaking these flints, the most important of them being that the angle of the flake scars bears a close resemblance to undoubted natural flaking and differs

Date	Sea-level	Climatic Phases	Archaeology	Sites	Geology
		POST-GLACIAL			
8000 B.C.			? Implements in East Anglia / UPPER PALAEOLITHIC		
	LOW	HUNSTANTON GLACIATION			Brown boulder clay
100,000					
	HIGH	IPSWICH INTERGLACIAL	LEVALLOISIAN	Bobbitshole, Ipswich Brundon	Bobbitshole Lake Beds / Brundon deposits
200,000					
	LOW	GIPPING GLACIATION			Gipping Till and Gravels
300,000					
	HIGH	HOXNE INTERGLACIAL	ACHEULIAN CLACTONIAN	Barnham High Lodge, Mildenhall Hoxne / Whitlingham	Hoxne Lake deposits / Nar Valley Beds
400,000					
	LOW / HIGH	LOWESTOFT GLACIATION			Lowestoft Till Corton Beds N. Sea Drift
500,000	LOW	CROMER INTERGLACIAL			Cromer Forest Bed
	HIGH	COLD PERIOD	? Implements in East Anglia		Norwich Crag Stone Bed Red Crag Bone Bed

(Archaeology column vertical labels spanning: PALAEOLITHIC, LOWER)

Chart B   *The Palaeolithic in East Anglia*

considerably from the human workmanship of later industries. It has been suggested that the chief cause of much of the flaking in the Norfolk Stone Bed was due to the grounding of floating pack-ice, jamming flints together on the floor of a shallow sea which was obviously uninhabitable. Other authorities, however, consider that the Bone and Stone Beds formed as beach deposits of weathered flints which were only gradually submerged by an encroaching sea and therefore were available for human occupation. Even so, the evidence is insufficient for anyone to assert with confidence the definite existence of Man in East Anglia before the advance of the first ice-sheets.

Slightly later in date are flint flakes found in crag sands at Foxhall, near Ipswich. These flakes come from an horizon which, it has been suggested, represents a shore line bordering the Crag Sea. These flints have been widely accepted as artifacts and certainly are more convincing than most of the Sub-Crag flints; but further material from this site is necessary before these objects can confidently be regarded as man-made tools, while their presence in the midst of a marine deposit requires a more satisfactory explanation. Another enigmatic industry termed the 'Cromerian', consisting of vast flint flakes with brilliant orange colouring found on the foreshore at Cromer and alleged to come from the Cromer Forest Bed, must also be regarded as of natural origin. This deposit was laid down during the first interglacial in this area, preceded by a cold period possibly represented by pack-ice in the Crag Sea.

The estuarine and freshwater deposits of the Cromer Forest Bed were formed in the delta of a great river, probably the Rhine, which here flowed in a northerly direction. Into this have been swept the bones and teeth of many species of animals, and it is clear from these that part of this period was warm. From pollen grains and the actual remains of trees, we may visualize in the area woodland of various types adapted to the climatic changes of this interglacial. In the colder conditions at the beginning and end of this period Scots pine and birch were the chief trees, while the intermediate warmer phase encouraged the growth of mixed-oak forest in which hornbeam, hazel, beech and elm were present. In the marshes, besides the alders, would be seen pond-weeds, sedges, water-lilies, mare's tail, and many other flowering plants still familiar in the British Isles. Only 5 per cent of the vegetation in these deposits is exotic or extinct, but a great contrast is apparent when the animals are considered, for the commonest species are now either extinct or denizens of warmer regions. Along the present coastline from Weybourne to Bacton and from Corton to Kessingland in Suffolk (the southern limit of this deposit) have come the remains of the southern elephant, the etruscan rhinoceros, hippopotamus, hyena, deer of several species, horse, voles and many other animals.

Much of the physical background of the Cromer Interglacial is thus well established, but Man and his tools are conspicuous by their absence. The estuarine nature of the beds has been held to account for this deficiency, but the absence of artifacts from the Forest Bed deposits is remarkable if Man was indeed living in the area at this time. One flint axe and a flint flake from Sidestrand, found in a glacial clay later than the Forest Bed, and not recovered under test conditions, have been used to bolster up the notion of Palaeolithic hunters preying on the rich fauna revealed by these deposits. But this evidence is too slender to be capable of proving such an assertion.

The Cromer Interglacial was ended by a major advance of the ice which moved across eastern Norfolk from north-west to south-east, depositing the greyish boulder clay or till so prominent in the cliffs of the Cromer area, and, farther south, the Norwich Brickearth, a yellowish brown or greyish sandy loam often known together as the 'North Sea Drift'. A second phase of this, the Lowestoft Glaciation, is indicated by the chalky boulder clay deposited by an ice sheet advancing from

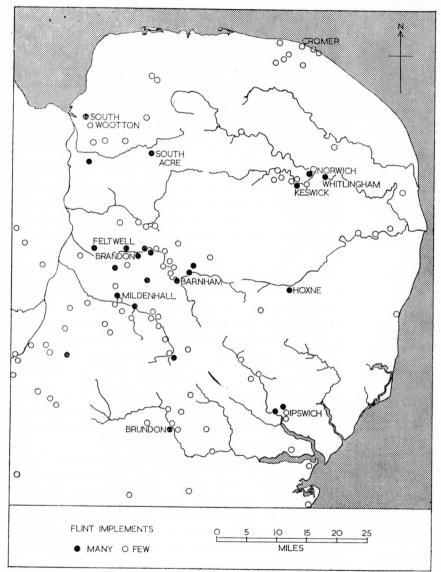

Fig. 2   Distribution of Lower Palaeolithic flint implements

the west over the whole of East Anglia and extending as far south as the old course of the River Thames. In between these two boulder clays lies a marine deposit, the Corton or Runton Sands, and from this, in the neighbourhood of Runton in north Norfolk, have been extracted small flint flakes with edge chipping, regarded by some as of human origin. These again may well be natural; their occurrence in a marine deposit does not strengthen the case for classifying them as artifacts.

It is thus not certain that East Anglia was inhabited before the beginning of the Second Interglacial period ushered in by the gradual melting of the ice of the Lowestoft Glaciation. Primitive handaxes made from nodules of flint, and flakes generally accepted to be of human origin, have been found in the Breckland gravels and are the oldest certain tools of Palaeo-lithic Man in East Anglia. Many of these flint axes are rolled and battered, but this in itself is no proof that their makers existed before the Lowestoft Glaciation.

Much is known of the vegetation and fauna of this Second, or Great, Interglacial (in East Anglia termed the Hoxne Inter-glacial, for the site of an extinct lake in that parish has yielded important evidence). This interglacial lasted perhaps 200,000 years, during which there was a sequence of climatic and vegetational changes starting with the sub-arctic conditions that followed the withdrawal of the Lowestoft ice-sheet, through a warm phase, warmer than today, to the cold conditions pre-ceding the onset of the Gipping Glaciation. The examination of pollen from Hoxne tells us that mixed-oak forest existed in the vicinity. It would be wrong to conceive of the whole of East Anglia as one vast forest, for patches of parkland broke the monotony. Here roamed the animals on which the small groups of hunters preyed—the straight-tusked elephant, rhinoceros, bison, horse and various species of deer.

A large population should not be assumed despite the

Fig. 2

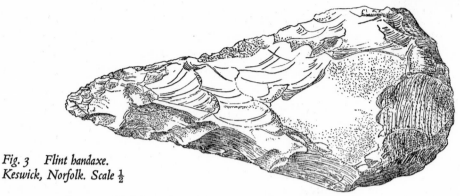

Fig. 3   Flint handaxe.
Keswick, Norfolk. Scale ½

numerous sites at which have been found tools of the Acheulian-Clactonian culture of this period, and despite the hundreds of tools which have been recovered from the best investigated of these sites, such as Hoxne, Whitlingham and Barnham. Several hundred flint tools can easily be produced by one family in a few days or weeks, and the implements from the sites we know have to be spread over tens of thousands of years. To judge from the habits of modern hunting groups, the whole of East Anglia at any moment in the Hoxne Interglacial was probably occupied by only a few families, each inhabiting a wide tract of forest and parkland across which they followed the seasonal movements of game. Temporary camping sites of these nomadic hunters, perhaps occupied at most for a few weeks or months, are indicated, at places like Hoxne, then on a lake shore, and Whitlingham on the slope of a river valley, by the concen-tration of flint tools. Here the bulk of the flint tools are as fresh as the day they fell from the knapper's hand, with little chemical alteration or physical abrasion. The principal tool from these and other sites is the pointed or almond-shaped handaxe, *Fig. 3* which probably served for cutting and scraping. These tools were made from flints obtained from outcrops of chalk or from earlier glacial beds. A nodule was struck with a hard hammer-stone and roughly flaked into shape, then smaller shallow flakes were knocked off the surface by blows from a bone or a hard wooden bar, thus producing a core tool. The waste flakes from these processes were often trimmed up; the smaller were probably used as knives, while the larger were converted into cleavers with an axe-like edge. These hunting groups had differing traditions in tool-making; most of them concentrated *Fig. 4* upon producing core-tools, the flakes from which had a wide, plain striking-platform. But the tools from a site like High Lodge, Mildenhall, were made principally from flakes, though they show by various technical details that their makers were in contact with the handaxe knappers. These discoveries indicate that we are dealing with a uniform culture with local variations. Although only stone tools normally survive, the discovery of the roughly pointed wooden spear of yew from Clacton-on-Sea, Essex, reminds us that a large part of the hunter's handiwork in making wooden tools and weapons has been lost to us, because conditions were not suitable for their preservation. There are signs that the forest was temporarily removed at this period in the Hoxne area, but it is uncertain whether this was due to the activities of Palaeolithic Man or a natural forest fire.

The climate again became colder as the ice-sheets of the Gipping Glaciation gradually advanced over East Anglia from the north-west. The Acheulian-Clactonian hunters retreated southward following the animals on which they preyed, leaving the tundra to the mammoth and woolly rhinoceros. After some thousands of years the climate again became warmer, the ice gradually melted and left behind the Gipping boulder clay and gravels containing tools from the preceding interglacial period which had been caught up by ice action.

The warmer period following the Gipping Glaciation is known in East Anglia as the Ipswich Interglacial, as deposits at Bobbitshole, near Ipswich, have been shown by pollen analysis to belong to this period. Contemporary deposits at

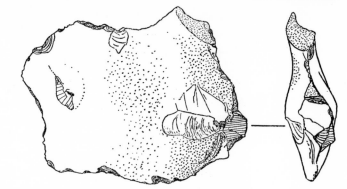

Fig. 4 Clactonian flint flake. Carrow, Norwich. Scale ½

Brundon, near Sudbury, have shown that this area was an open grassy plain with patches of mixed forest, in which hornbeam was common. At the height of the Interglacial, summers were probably warmer and winters drier than today. When the area was largely open grassland, the hunters would have encountered mammoth, rhinoceros, bison, an occasional lion and herds of wild horses. In the neighbouring woods lurked many deer, both red and the large Irish species, the formidable aurochs, bear, wild pig and wolf. In ponds and marshes dwelt the European freshwater tortoise, frogs and water-voles.

The general way of life of the hunters who came into East Anglia during the Ipswich Interglacial was probably similar to that of their predecessors, but their tool types were somewhat different. Survivors of the Acheulian tradition were still making that general purpose tool, the handaxe, but now it was thinner, smaller, often heart-shaped, and usually made from a flake instead of a nodule. But other groups, though perhaps influenced by the Acheulian-Clactonian culture, developed a distinctive tool form of their own. This is known as the Levallois flake, which was trimmed into shape while still attached to the parent nodule. When removed from the core by a bone or wooden punch hit by a wooden or stone hammer, the flake was immediately ready for use as a knife without further trimming.

Fig. 5

37

Its striking platform is typically faceted from this preliminary dressing. Trimming the edge converted some flakes into serviceable skin scrapers.

The Ipswich Interglacial lasted perhaps 60,000 years, only about one-third as long as the Hoxne Interglacial. It was brought to an end by a further glaciation lasting for about 100,000 years. During this final glaciation the ice advanced and retreated several times, though only one advance reached as far south as East Anglia. To this is usually attributed, at between 20,000 and 30,000 B.C., the deposition of the Hunstanton, or reddish-brown, boulder clay which has been recognized along a coastal strip of north-west Norfolk. At the time of the Hunstanton Glaciation, mammoth, woolly rhinoceros and reindeer roamed the tundra to the south of the actual ice sheets, while Man is notably absent, perhaps owing to the lack of caves in the area. The presence of roaming bands of hunters in Wales, south-west England and the southern Pennines at this period can be deduced from discoveries of flint, bone and antler tools, though the evidence so far produced from East Anglia does not prove that hunters penetrated the area during the slightly warmer phases between the periods of most intense cold. Flint scrapers, blades, graving tools and waste cores have been claimed to come from the Hunstanton boulder clay and would, if con-temporary, be of Upper Palaeolithic date. This is not impossible, but the form of the tools suggests that they are more likely to belong to the ensuing Mesolithic Age. Similarly, a whole series of tools from a brickfield at Dales Road, Ipswich, has also been claimed as Upper Palaeolithic but these, from the pottery associated with them, are clearly of Neolithic date.

Fig. 5   Levallois flint flake.
Brundon, Sudbury, Suffolk.
Scale about ½

Somewhat more convincing are four laurel-leaf-shaped flint blades reputed to have been found with reindeer bones beneath eight feet of gravel at Constantine Road, Ipswich, and another from gravel at Bury St Edmunds. These are similar in appearance to blades of the Solutrean culture of Upper Palaeolithic date on the continent, but they have been found nowhere else in Britain under conditions which guarantee that they are of this period rather than of the Neolithic. It is clear that many of the archaeological finds attributed to this period must now be rejected, and others placed in a suspense account pending further investigation.

We have so far said nothing about the physical appearance of the Palaeolithic hunters in the area, and for the very sound reason that no unequivocal remains of their skeletons have yet been recognized. Human bones from Hunstanton, Norfolk, and Ipswich and Westley, Suffolk, have been published as of Palaeolithic date, but the application to them of modern scientific methods, like the fluorine test, has shown that they are later than, and not contemporary with, the deposits in which they are alleged to have been found. It is unfortunate that in the case of the human jaw found in a Crag pit at Foxhall, near Ipswich, in 1855 and later taken to the United States, its subsequent disappearance prevents us from coming to a definite conclusion. The level from which it came is likewise unrecorded, though its organic content was similar to that of animal bones from an horizon in the Red Crag associated with flint flakes, as mentioned above. But if it really came from this deposit it would be just as difficult to explain as the flint flakes also claimed as being of human origin. From a surviving drawing, this jaw looks almost completely modern with a strongly projecting chin, but it possesses in its double mental foramen a primitive feature rarely found in modern man. Though the antiquity of the Foxhall jaw and its associations must remain debatable, its existence should not be forgotten, in the hope that one day more bones of a similar creature will be unearthed under test conditions.

Despite the somewhat cavalier manner in which we have swept aside these alleged Palaeolithic human remains from East Anglia, we can hazard a guess as to the appearance of the hunters living there in the Hoxne Interglacial, for fragments of a human skull have been found at Swanscombe, Kent, with Acheulian handaxes contemporaneous with those from East Anglia. The Swanscombe skull fragments are almost indis-tinguishable from those of modern man and we shall therefore not be far wrong if we regard our East Anglian Acheulian hunters as long-headed, probably dark-haired, individuals, not noticeably dissimilar from some types still surviving in the British Isles.

Fig. 2

At the beginning of this chapter we drew attention to the vast length of the Palaeolithic Age. The map showing the distribution of the tools of Lower Palaeolithic Man is some-what misleading, in that both the relics of the temporary camps of minute groups of hunters and incidental losses over hundreds of thousands of years are shown together. Any attempt to evaluate the distribution is also vitiated by our ignorance of the topography of the area in each interglacial, and by the fortuitous distribution of modern sand, gravel and clay pits which have revealed most of the known sites. Nevertheless, with the ex-ception of finds on the Cromer-Holt ridge, a scatter on the Fen edge and the heaths of west Norfolk, it is notable that the vast majority of Palaeolithic discoveries come from valley gravels. This may be seen by the concentrations in the Norwich area, in the lower Waveney valley, in the Little Ouse, Thet, Wissey and Lark valleys in Breckland, and in the Gipping valley near Ipswich and the Stour valley in the vicinity of Sudbury.

CHAPTER III

The Mesolithic

ABOUT 8000 B.C. the cold climate of Late-Glacial times evolved into the milder, though still cold, conditions of the Pre-Boreal. This phase, with the succeeding Boreal and Atlantic phases, lasted until about 2500 B.C. These conventional dates for the duration of the Mesolithic are necessarily somewhat arbitrary, though increasingly supported by radiocarbon dating.

From 8000 to 7000 B.C. there was a gradual and rapid rise of temperature to about 12 degrees Centigrade in the summer, though this peak was still about 2½ degrees lower than the average July temperature of today. The dwarf birch and willow copses of the Late-Glacial tundra were replaced by forests of birch and pine. Eastern England was still joined to the continent and much of what is now the southern part of the North Sea was then freshwater fen and lagoons ('Northsealand'). The mammoth and the woolly rhinoceros, which had roamed East Anglia during the Last Glaciation, had now retreated to the far north or become extinct, but herds of reindeer and wild horse survived, together with the arctic hare, fox and white grouse. With the spread of woodland came the forest-loving animals—red deer, wild pig, wild cat and badger.

We have seen in the previous chapter that the Upper Palaeolithic hunters have left few unequivocal traces of their presence in East Anglia. Their immediate successors in the first phase of the Mesolithic are equally elusive. It is true that flint industries at numerous East Anglian sites are attributed to the Mesolithic, but almost all are ill-explored, found on the modern surface, or in deposits unsuitable for the preservation of pollen or organic material. Thus, at most sites, the classification is typological but not necessarily chronological. Until stratified sites are discovered and excavated, it is impossible to do more than suggest the survival of Upper Palaeolithic hunters and the arrival of fresh immigrants from what is now the continent. A tanged flint flake, probably an arrowhead, found at Cranwich, Norfolk, which is similar to those of the Upper Palaeolithic Hamburg culture of north-western Germany and the Early Mesolithic cultures of adjacent areas, tends to support this view.

Fortunately, the evidence for the human occupation of East Anglia in the second phase of the Mesolithic, from about 7000 to 5000 B.C., is slightly more convincing. During this Boreal phase, the climate was continental in type, with a low rainfall and an average summer temperature at the end of the phase of 17 degrees Centigrade, about 2½ degrees higher than today. Birch or pine remained the dominant trees in the extensive forests, with hazel becoming increasingly abundant, though alder and mixed-oak forest began to colonize suitable heavy soils towards the end of the phase.

At the beginning of the Boreal phase East Anglia was still linked to the continent, and 'Northsealand' was still largely freshwater fen. But a rising sea soon gained mastery over this plain and by about 6000 B.C. much of it was submerged, though Britain only became an island about 1000 years later. Before this decisive event took place, eastern England lay wide open to influences from Denmark, southern Sweden and northern Germany, where the Maglemosian culture was centred, and hunters of this group had reached British soil before the end of the Pre-Boreal. The intervening 'Northsealand' was occupied during the first centuries of the Boreal, as was confirmed by an accidental discovery in 1931. The Lowestoft trawler *Colinda* was fishing between the Leman and Ower Banks, some twenty-five miles north-east of Cromer, and dredged a lump of peaty material called 'moorlog' from the sea bottom at a depth of about 120 feet. The lump was casually broken on deck before being cast back into the sea and from it

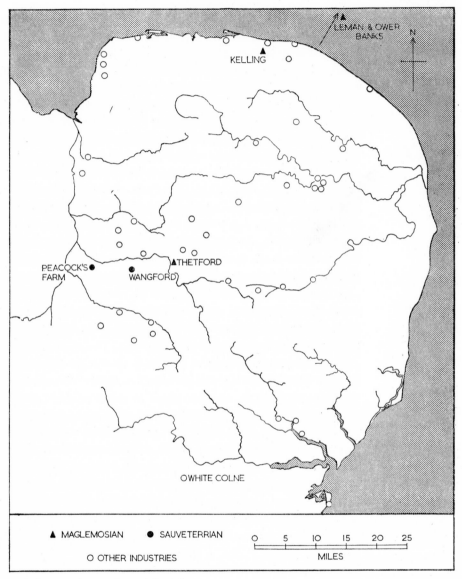

LEMAN & OWER
BANKS

N

KELLING

PEACOCK'S
FARM

WANGFORD

THETFORD

WHITE COLNE

▲ MAGLEMOSIAN   ● SAUVETERRIAN

O OTHER INDUSTRIES

0   5   10   15   20   25

MILES

Fig. 6   Distribution of Mesolithic cultures

Plate 4

fell a barbed bone point of red deer antler. A comparison with similar objects in the Baltic area found embedded in the skeletons of pike makes it clear that this also was the prong of a fish spear. Later examination of this 'moorlog' by the C14 technique has suggested a date of 6500 B.C. for the formation of the peat.

Fig. 6

Flint implements characteristic of the Maglemosian culture have been found at Kelling in north Norfolk and at Two Mile Bottom, Thetford, in the south-west of that county, but probably many other sites could be added if the full range of their flint products was known. These two sites have yielded vast numbers of small, narrow flint flakes, the waste products of knapping,

Fig. 7

together with the rarer, irregular microliths or flakes blunted on one or both edges. These latter would have been set in wooden hafts and used for boring or cutting. Other flakes were left un-trimmed, but had clearly been utilized before being discarded. Scrapers, borers, burins and core axes with a tranchet cutting

Fig. 8

edge, made by the intersection of two or more flake surfaces, also formed an integral part of the industry. The presence of cutting tools like the axe indicates that these people were making use of timber from their forest environment.

From discoveries made in the Baltic area a general picture can be obtained of the Maglemosian culture. We must en-visage small, highly mobile groups of hunters, who covered considerable distances in the course of a year, establishing temporary camps while engaged in the pursuit of forest animals, fish or fowl, according to season. Their main food supply probably came from the aurochs and elk, red and roe deer and wild pig; the dog, which first appeared in western Europe at this time, was doubtless invaluable for hunting these forest mammals. Food from this source was supplemented by fishing with barbed spears in inland waters, where the pike was the

Fig. 7   Microlith. principal victim. Fishing nets with bark floats, wicker fish-
Hevingham, Norfolk. traps and bone fish-hooks are also known, while the remains of
Scale 2/1 dug-out wooden canoes and broad-bladed wooden paddles are

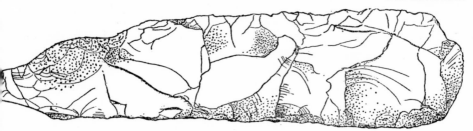

Fig. 8   Tranchet flint axehead. Carrow, Norwich. Scale ½

evidence for navigation in sheltered waterways. Various species of duck, swan and goose were probably shot with bow and arrow or snared, while smaller mammals like hare, badger, otter and fox, were hunted for their fur.

The temporary camps of these Maglemosian hunters were usually in river valleys, on eminences in low plains or close to the shores of lakes, as at Hockham and Wretham in south-west Norfolk. Kelling, on the other hand, lies high on dry sandy heathland far from an obvious water-supply. The restricted area of these camps (Kelling occupies about 60 by 50 yards and Hockham about 200 by 50 yards) suggests the presence of only a few families living there for a few weeks, or, at most, months.

The Maglemosians were not the only inhabitants of East Anglia during the Boreal phase, for there were also members of another cultural group, the Sauveterrian (previously called Tardenoisian), named after the French site now regarded as typical. This culture is marked by an absence of axes, adzes and similar wood-cutting equipment, and by the presence of microliths of geometric forms like trapezes, crescents and triangles which were attached to darts and spears. These micro-liths are often minute, few being over an inch in length and some as small as one-quarter of an inch.

As the Sauveterrian folk lived in treeless localities, they had no need for heavy tools for felling and working timber. Their traces can be found at sites on the sand-dunes bordering the

*Fig. 9
Geometric microlith.
Wangford, north-
west Suffolk.
Scale 2/1*

45

Fens, as at Wangford in north-west Suffolk, and Peacock's Farm, Shippea Hill, just over the border into Cambridgeshire. It is still uncertain whether this culture was a native British development from one of the Upper Palaeolithic hunting groups or whether it had evolved in France and Belgium and been introduced to Britain. Neither do we know when the distinctive material equipment associated with it first developed; but in East Anglia at least, from the evidence of the peat in which the microliths were found at Peacock's Farm, it is clear that the Sauveterrians were living in the area before the end of the Boreal phase, that is, before about 5000 B.C.

Hunters of both the Maglemosian and Sauveterrian cultures possibly erected flimsy tents for use during the summer. It seems probable that the Maglemosians, at least, constructed more substantial shelters as winter quarters. An inadequately published discovery at White Colne in north Essex suggests that irregular-shaped dwellings, roofed with boughs and sods and suitable for three or four persons, were devised by hunters of this culture. Here two pits, each eight feet across and four feet deep, had been scooped out of the gravel with a small hearth between; judging by the associated flint industry, they belonged to the Maglemosian culture.

The third and last phase of the Mesolithic began about 5000 B.C., when the warm, dry continental climate of the Boreal gave place to the warm and moist oceanic conditions of the Atlantic phase. In the North Sea the water-level continued to rise throughout this phase, though less rapidly than in the Boreal. The heavier rainfall and greater warmth stimulated the growth of deciduous forests of which the oak, elm and lime were the most prominent members. In these woodlands dwelt red and roe deer, wild pig and aurochs, but the reindeer had now completely disappeared.

Both the Maglemosian and Sauveterrian cultures probably continued in East Anglia during the Atlantic phase, when the denser forests impeded movement more than did the coniferous forests of the Boreal; thus the material culture of the hunters of this last phase tended to develop on local lines. A group of sites in the Wensum valley at Hellesdon (Norwich), Sparham and Lyng, all within easy reach of an adequate water-supply, can probably be attributed to this last phase of the Mesolithic between about 5000 and 2500 B.C. Only the flint industry survives, and this is characterized by conical and double-ended cores from which numerous narrow flakes were struck, some being trimmed to form non-geometric microliths. Core axes were still being produced, some in the form of long and narrow picks known as 'Thames Picks', an example of which has been found at Heacham. But many flint axes with the tranchet type of cutting edge already noted, were now made from flakes instead of cores.

In common with almost the whole of Britain, East Anglia has so far produced no definite physical remains of its Mesolithic occupants, and consequently we have no evidence as to their burial customs. The only skeletal material from East Anglia which may be of Mesolithic date, is a skull found in 1954 in the bank of the River Yare at Strumpshaw, Norfolk. The closest parallels to it come from burials of undoubted Mesolithic date on the Island of Téviec in Brittany, but there is no direct evidence for dating this Strumpshaw skull, and, if Mesolithic, it has certainly been re-deposited at the site at which it was found.

It should be emphasized that our picture of the life of these nomadic food-gatherers is very incomplete, and must remain so until the discovery and excavation of many new camping sites, on soils suitable for the preservation of organic materials, places the vital evidence in our hands.

CHAPTER IV

The Neolithic

W HILE THE EARLIER Mesolithic hunters were eking out a precarious existence in East Anglia, or were crossing the freshwater fens of 'Northsealand', events of great importance were taking place in the Middle East, the repercussions of which were ultimately to revolutionize world economy and pave the way for the development of civilization.

At least as early as 7000 B.C., some of the inhabitants of the plains of the Middle East had discovered how to cultivate cereals and domesticate sheep and goats, as recent excavations at Jericho have shown. Not only did the augmented food supply enable a larger population than before to settle, more or less permanently, in the areas once roamed over by small hunting groups, but it also provided the leisure necessary for the develop/ ment of a richer culture. Emigrants from the Middle East carried the idea of food production to the Mesolithic food gatherers of Europe, when these early farmers were forced to move under the twin spurs of soil exhaustion and over/ population. The Neolithic peasants travelled up the Danube valley to reach the plains of north/western Europe, and by boat along the shores of the Mediterranean to France and the Iberian Peninsula. The earliest agriculturalists in the Low Countries arrived there by the Danube route some time before 4000 B.C., but penetrated no farther west. Despite the proximity of Britain to the Netherlands, it was not till about 2500 B.C. that the first Neolithic farmers reached southern England. From settle/ ments in the Low Countries some farmers ultimately made their way across the North Sea to eastern England, taking with them their seed/corn and domestic animals. At about the same time, more numerous groups of settlers from northern France were making their landfall on the south coast and spreading on to

Culture	Origin	Phase I 2500 B.C.	Phase II ? 1900	Phase III 1700
Mesolithic survival	——			
Windmill Hill	N. France and Low Countries			
Rinyo-Clacton	Local development			
Peterborough	Local development			
Bell Beaker	Holland and Middle Rhine			
Corded Ware	Holland or N.W. Germany			
Rusticated Ware	? Local development			
Necked Beaker	Local development			

Chart C *Chart of Neolithic Cultures*

the chalk downs. The culture of these earliest farmers is known, from the type site in Wiltshire, as the Windmill Hill or Neo-lithic A culture. In East Anglia, the Neolithic Age may be regarded as lasting from about 2500 B.C. to about 1700 B.C., and can be divided into three chronological phases.

We saw in the last chapter that Mesolithic East Anglia was sparsely occupied by small groups of hunters and fishers. Many of these could not be attributed with any certainty to the two principal cultures, and it may well be that some of the rather indeterminate flint industries are contemporary with Phase I of the Neolithic. Certainly the distribution of these Mesolithic sites is complementary to those of the Windmill Hill culture as at present known. The latter are concentrated in Breckland, particularly on the sandhills bordering the Fens, on the chalk ridge of west Norfolk, in the Ipswich area and on a few sites in east Norfolk where the soil is sandy. The sparse vegetation of these areas could have been easily cleared by the first Neolithic farmers when establishing plots for the cultivation of wheat or

Fig. 10

49

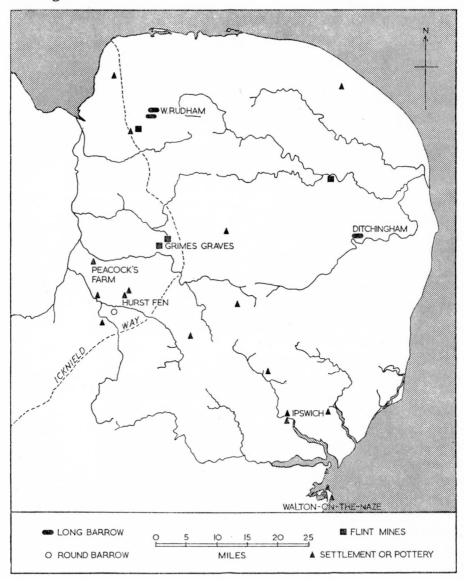

Fig. 10   Distribution of Windmill Hill (Neolithic A) culture

barley. Their other main activity was the herding of oxen and sheep; there seems little trace of pig-keeping in East Anglia at this date, although it is important elsewhere. There is ample evidence that the Breckland woods sheltered numerous red deer of considerable size and some roe deer, as well as wild boar, the aurochs and many small animals.

Nothing is yet known of houses in East Anglia during this phase of the Windmill Hill culture, but evidence from the ensuing phase suggests that relatively small rectangular timber-framed buildings were being built. The principal remains of the culture in Phase I consist of fragments of plain, dark-faced pottery, technically of high quality. Forms commonly found are bag-shaped pots, bowls and cups, often with rolled-over rims. The most important site at which this pottery has yet been found is Peacock's Farm, near Shippea Hill, Cambridgeshire, where it occurred in the Lower Peat and thus could be dated by pollen analysis. Similar pottery has also been found at several sites in the Mildenhall area, at Edingthorpe in north-east Norfolk and in the flint mines at Grime's Graves, Weeting. Flint was the chief raw material for tools and weapons, the most important of which was the hafted axe. Several hundreds of these have been found in East Anglia, unfortunately usually isolated, so that they may well belong to any phase of this period or even the Early Bronze Age. These core axeheads were chipped into shape, and sometimes given a keener edge by polishing on a block of stone, such as the block of quartzite found with a group of axes at Lound, Suffolk. The leaf-shaped arrowheads associated with this culture in East Anglia are very common, indicating that the pursuit of game was still vital to the economy. Other common flint tools were scrapers, knives, choppers and hammers, which, like the axes and arrowheads, were introduced by the newcomers and not copied from those of the Mesolithic hunters in adjacent areas.

Despite claims to a greater antiquity, the systematic exploitation

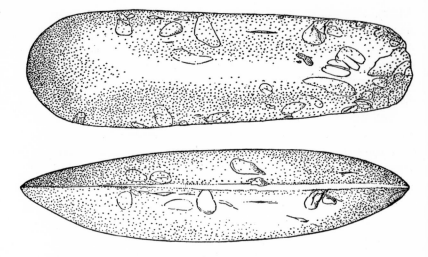

Fig. 11   Polished flint axehead. Feltwell, Norfolk. Scale ½

of the flint resources of East Anglia by mining into the chalk was inaugurated by men of the Windmill Hill culture in Phase I, though the greatest development occurred in Phase II. The great flint mining site of Grime's Graves in south-west Norfolk owes its prestige to its considerable extent (some 366 shafts having been identified) and to the scale on which it has been explored. But this was not the only group of flint mines in East Anglia, for others have been recognized at Lynford near by, at Great Massingham, and at Whitlingham near Norwich, and more may possibly be discovered.

The mines at Grime's Graves range from simple open-cast pits, 10–15 feet deep, to shafts cut through sand and chalk to a depth of 30 feet with radiating galleries linking one shaft with another. As each fresh pit was excavated, the waste material was dumped in the galleries and shafts of pits previously exhausted. Polished axes and the antlers of red deer, used as levers, have been more commonly found in the galleried mines,

Plate 6

while tools made from the leg bones of oxen occur more frequently in the simple pits. It would seem probable that the different types of mine are all broadly contemporary, and that the particular mining technique employed in each pit is related to the depth at which the best quality flint—the 'floorstone'— occurs. The risks inherent in sinking deep shafts with galleries are shown by the discovery of a miner's skeleton in one of the galleries at Whitlingham in the eighteenth century. Apart from the danger of the gallery roof collapsing on the miner, there was always the possibility that the several weeks' labour involved in sinking a deep pit might prove fruitless, owing to the poverty of the floorstone at that spot. Such was the situation in Pit 15 at Grime's Graves, where a marked deficiency of flint was associated with a remarkable ritual assemblage. By the entrance to a gallery, a pedestal of chalk blocks was surmounted by the roughly carved chalk figurine of a pregnant female, with, close by, a number of chalk balls and a carved phallus. In the centre of the pit was an 'altar' of flint blocks on which seven deer-antler picks had been laid. In front of the altar stood a chalk cup of the type used elsewhere in the mines as lamps. The only reasonable interpretation of this dramatic arrangement is that it represents a shrine of the Earth Goddess, dedicated by a group of miners (perhaps seven in number) to ensure a more abundant supply of flint in the next shaft to be sunk. Around the mine shafts lay hundreds of 'working floors', on which the knappers trimmed the flint nodules into the shape of axes. These axes were presumably traded from this factory unfinished, and the final flaking and sharpening was probably executed by the customer, who may have collected them from the mine-head or received them through the agency of a middleman. The range of distribution of the Grime's Graves axes is unknown, but the existence of other flint mines in East Anglia suggests that its products were largely for local use, particularly for forest clearance.

Plate 7

Plate 9

Fig. 12 Leaf-shaped flint arrowhead. Santon, Norfolk. Actual size

No houses for the miners have yet been detected, and the absence of a water-supply would have prevented permanent occupation; though they certainly cooked meals on the site and lit fires in the partly infilled shafts of disused mines. The whole of the mining at Grime's Graves may well have occupied the energies of a mere handful of miners for a few centuries. Though it is conceivable that neighbouring villagers visited the site and occasionally sank a pit, the expert skill displayed in the construction and exploitation of the galleried shafts indicates the presence of full-time craftsmen. These were doubtless specialists in mining and knapping who depended for their food and their supply of antler picks on local farmers and hunters.

The origins of the Windmill Hill culture in East Anglia are elusive. It is suggested that in this area there met and fused two cultural strains derived from the Netherlands, northern Germany and Denmark on the one hand, and from northern France via southern England and the Icknield Way route on the other. How much influence should be attributed to each strain is not at present clear. Though most of the early East Anglian Windmill Hill pottery bears a general resemblance to that from Wessex, the rolled rims are not commonly found there, and the carinated bowls, like those from Peacock's Farm, are better paralleled in Belgium, which also provides excellent analogies for the East Anglian flint-mining industries and for leaf arrowheads. It is tempting to suggest that the inhabitants of the sites on the margins of Breckland and Fenland came from Wessex, while the geographical position of sites like Walton-on-the-Naze, Edingthorpe and Whitlingham, argues strongly for the arrival there of immigrant farmers and miners from the Low Countries.

If Phase I of the Neolithic presents a large number of problems, Phase II positively bristles with them, as indications of no less than four cultures can be detected in East Anglia. In addition to the Windmill Hill culture, three fresh groups, the

Rinyo-Clacton, Peterborough and Bell-Beaker cultures, can be recognized, principally from their distinctive pottery. The dividing line between Phases I and II is somewhat indefinite, but the end of Phase II is clearly defined in the southern Fens by a marine clay deposit, indicating an extensive and rapid sub-sidence. Archaeological material of all the cultures mentioned has been found sealed beneath the clays of Fenland or on the shore of north-east Essex, though here the transgression may have been later. Other archaeological finds, probably of this period, have been found on the foreshore of north-west Norfolk below the high-water mark, suggesting a loss of land which had been occupied up to this time.

The development of the Windmill Hill culture during Phase II is characterized by pottery, termed Mildenhall Ware, from the quantity found on sites in that parish. A common type is a bowl with a large rim joined to a shoulder of similar size by a nearly vertical neck, and often bearing close-set vertical or oblique channelling. Pottery of this type has been found at Hurst Fen ⟶ Plate 3 and Hayland House, Mildenhall, and at Eriswell; at Kesteven Road and Dales Road, in Ipswich, and at Martlesham near by, as well as various other sites. On the Essex coast it has been shown to be later stratigraphically than the undecorated wares of Phase I. The flint industries on these sites consist of cores and thousands of flakes from which scrapers and leaf arrowheads were made. Saddle querns, used for grinding corn, were shaped ⟶ Plate 5 from large nodules of quartzite, diorite or flint. Excavations at Hurst Fen have revealed post-holes of rectangular timber-framed houses, but how far these may be regarded as typical of the rest of East Anglia is as yet unknown. Traces of structures were found at both Kesteven Road and Dales Road, but these were not sufficiently explored to reveal their significance.

As the population increased in Phase II, it became necessary to expand the area for cultivation and grazing. In Breckland and adjacent areas this led to the progressive clearance of some of the deciduous woodland, as the primitive type of agriculture practised by the Windmill Hill people quickly exhausted the thin soils. This deforestation was carried out by the 'slash and burn' technique, when the trees were felled with flint or stone axes and the stumps burned. An analysis of the pollen pre-served in the lake muds at the former Hockham Mere in north-east Breckland shows a great expansion in the amount derived from grasses, ling and herbs, indicating forest clearance soon after the transition from the Atlantic to the Sub-Boreal phases corresponding probably to Phase II, though it may have begun in Phase I. The presence of the pollen of agricultural weeds, such as ribwort plantain, strikingly demonstrates this extension of farming. The grazing of domestic animals would have assisted in preventing the regeneration of the former dense wood-land on abandoned plots, thus creating the Breckland heaths.

A somewhat casual attitude to the dead is indicated by the use of a human femur as a pick at Grime's Graves. This con-clusion is strengthened by the discovery in other shafts of a girl's skeleton and other fragmentary human bones, apparently thrown in with the chalk rubble.

Apart from these scattered finds indicating the disposal, rather than the burial, of the dead, there is little evidence from East Anglia of the burial rites of the Windmill Hill people, other than three long barrows and an enigmatic mound. The long barrows lie on West Rudham and Harpley Commons close to the Icknield Way, and on Broome Heath, Ditchingham, in the Waveney valley. Pottery of Windmill Hill type has been discovered on the surface of the mounds at Ditchingham and Harpley, but only the West Rudham barrow has been excavated. Contrary to expectation, no group of inhumations was found inside this mound which is 216 feet long and 60 feet wide. Evidence was found near the south end which suggested that the bodies had instead been burned on a prepared platform of gravel, which was subsequently covered with turf and more gravel after the pyre had cooled. Similar materials were used to cover a ditch-encircled area on the south side of the mound, where a pit and gutter suggest that libations formed part of the funeral rites. The cremation ritual at West Rudham is paralleled in unchambered long barrows in central Wessex, and the position of the West Rudham barrow has not unnaturally suggested a diffusion of the idea from Wessex along the Icknield Way. Other possible analogies to the cremation ritual in long barrows may, however, be found in Belgium. The location of the Ditchingham barrow, so close to the East Coast, may also point to the derivation of the unchambered long barrow from across the North Sea. The enigmatic mound referred to above, probably a round barrow, is situated at Worlington, Suffolk, and formed the eccentric core of a later Bronze Age round barrow called Swale's Tumulus. In the original mound, some 35 feet in diameter, signs of an extensive fire and cremated bones were found, suggesting that a body had been burnt on a pyre. North of the margin of this mound a grave had been cut which contained charred oak boards, possibly from a bier or coffin, with cremated bone fragments, burnt flints, potsherds and half a polished flint axehead. This isolated example of individual interment, alien to the usual Windmill Hill tradition, is at present unique in East Anglia.

It is clear that a much more intensive investigation of the Windmill Hill culture in East Anglia in Phase II is necessary before its origins can be determined. The similarity of its pottery to the Abingdon group of the Middle Thames area, and the affinities of the West Rudham long barrow with Wessex might be interpreted as a diffusion north-eastwards from that area along the Icknield Way. However, the distribution of Mildenhall Ware, concentrated in Breckland, the Ipswich region and the adjacent Essex coast, and not found farther south-west than Bedfordshire and Buckinghamshire, suggests that the culture is more likely to have been a regional development in East

Anglia, supplemented by elements from across the North Sea.
In Phase I the Windmill Hill farmers had shared East
Anglia with the survivors of the Mesolithic peoples, to whom
they had introduced the notions of hoe⁄cultivation and the
herding of domestic animals. The fusion of these two traditions
gave rise to the Secondary Neolithic cultures in Phases II and III,
called, after their type sites, 'Peterborough' and 'Rinyo⁄Clacton'.

The Peterborough culture is distinguished by coarse, heavy,
round⁄based pottery with thickened rims and profuse decoration,
produced by impressing twisted cord, the human finger⁄nail or
leg⁄bones of birds. This pottery is widely distributed over
southern England and more sparsely in East Anglia. Sites
occur in Breckland, including Grime's Graves and Ickburgh in
the Norfolk portion and Barnham, Honington and Icklingham
in north⁄west Suffolk. Characteristic pottery has also been
found at Edingthorpe in north⁄east Norfolk, lying in a hollow
which may form part of a habitation, in the Ipswich region and
on the Essex coast. The Peterborough folk made and used flint
and stone axes, flint knives with polished edges, curved flint
sickles (for cutting corn or reeds), and two types of arrowhead,
one leaf⁄shaped and the other with chisel⁄edges (tranchet). It is
probable that the miners at Grime's Graves included some of
these people, and that they contributed the Mesolithic features
apparent in the flint⁄working techniques at that site, as well as
Plate 8   the scratchings of red deer on flint crust.

Although in East Anglia flint axes were most commonly
used because of the vast local natural resources of this material,
axes of igneous rocks were preferred for their superior durability.
In the last few years, many of the stone axes found in this region
have been sliced and examined in an attempt to determine the
source of the raw material. Only a fraction of the available axes
has yet been studied, but important results have already emerged.
It is probable that at least half may have been made locally
from erratic rocks collected from glacial deposits, but the rest

have clearly been imported into East Anglia. About one-third of the igneous axes studied can confidently be assigned to definite axe-factories or restricted areas in other parts of Britain, whence they were traded to many parts of the country. Impor-tant sources exploited in the Neolithic include Cornwall, south-west Wales, Graig Lwyd near Penmaenmawr in North Wales, Great Langdale in the Lake District and probably Teesdale. Ceremonial axes of jadeite were also imported, possibly from Brittany. It is uncertain when this trade began, but by Phase II Great Langdale axes were being imported to the Windmill Hill site at Hurst Fen, Mildenhall, and to many sites in Norfolk, while Cornish axes were traded to the inhabitants of the Ipswich region and of the Essex coast. It is to the wandering herdsmen of the Secondary Neolithic cultures that this trade owes its expansion in this and the ensuing phase.

Fig. 13

The Peterborough folk were, then, traders as well as stock-raisers, hunters and flint miners, and possibly, at times, corn-growers. Evidences of their local Mesolithic ancestry can be seen in their heavy flint industry of picks and tranchet axes, together with scrapers on blades, borers and tranchet arrow-heads, and in the artistic tradition displayed in their crude drawings at Grime's Graves. They owed their farming know-ledge to their Windmill Hill neighbours, and the idea of pottery-making, but its form and decoration were their own distinctive contribution.

The Rinyo-Clacton culture in southern England can be distinguished by its flat-bottomed pots, lavishly ornamented with triangles or lozenges, incised or grooved, or outlined by irregular ridges. Sites of this culture have been found on the Essex coast, and in Wessex as far north as the Cotswolds and the Middle Thames; in East Anglia they have been identified in the Ipswich region (Creeting St Mary), in Breckland (Honington) and in north-east Norfolk (West Runton and Edingthorpe). At Edingthorpe a fragment of this pottery was

Fig. 14

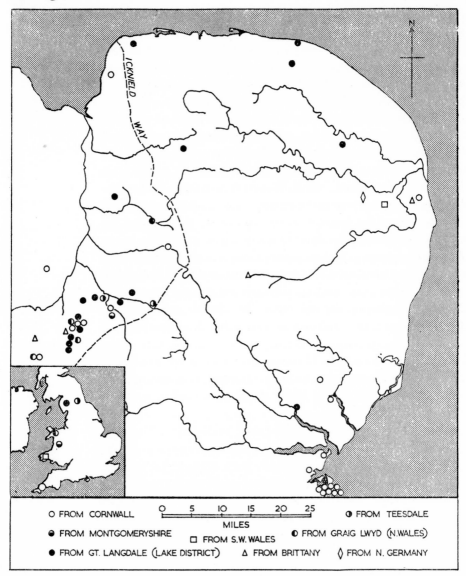

Fig. 13   Distribution of imported stone tools

found apparently discarded before any Peterborough folk visited the site, but at Honington the Peterborough folk arrived first, thus showing that people of both cultures lived in this area at the same time, presumably on peaceful terms. Excavation at Honington suggested that the Rinyo⁄Clacton folk lived in oval huts with pits or cooking holes outside.

The flint industry associated with Rinyo⁄Clacton sites is a light one, in which tranchet arrowheads predominate, though leaf arrowheads are also found; serrated flakes and scrapers are common. Little is known of the economy of these people from East Anglian evidence, but in Wessex they concentrated on the herding of swine, with cattle⁄tending of secondary importance. The origins of the Rinyo⁄Clacton culture in East Anglia are at present obscure. Its flint industry owes something to its Mesolithic ancestry, and its pottery designs and technique may represent the translation into clay of traditional local Mesolithic work in wood and basketry. Though the designs on some of the pots could be derived from the Iberian peninsula or western France, the finger⁄tip or finger⁄pinched rustication of its ornament suggests a connexion with Holland; this, how⁄ever, has been disputed. There the matter must rest until fresh evidence comes to light, bearing in mind that this culture continued through Phase III of the local Neolithic into the Early Bronze Age.

The first members of the final group included in Phase II,

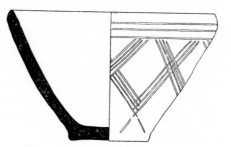

Fig. 14 Rinyo⁄Clacton pottery bowl. West Runton, Norfolk. Scale ¼

Plate 10

the Bell Beaker culture, had settled in East Anglia by *c.* 2000 B.C., probably before the submergence in the Fens. The characteristic pot of this culture is a thin and well-made beaker of shallow S-profile, ornamented in zones bordered by horizontal dentated lines made with a comb or bearing the impress of twined cord. Most of the bell beakers known from East Anglia are isolated finds, probably for domestic use, but some probably come from flat inhumation graves, though soil acidity has often destroyed all trace of the human skeleton. Bodies were normally buried in a flexed position, as instanced by the skeletons of a woman and child found with three bell beakers in a flat grave at Brantham, Suffolk. Occasionally, however, a small round barrow was erected over the body with its beaker, as at Cley-next-the-Sea, but this practice may belong in time to Phase III and reflect the influence of the intrusive Corded Ware culture. The principal weapon of the Bell Beaker folk for war and the chase was the bow. Stone guards, which protected the archer's wrist from the recoil of the bow string, such as the one found at Brandon, Suffolk, and the many barbed and tanged flint arrowheads, support this view.

Nothing is yet known of any structural features of Bell Beaker settlements in East Anglia. It is probable that these were temporary camps suited to the stock-breeding activities of a predominantly pastoral people, who may well have used tents similar to those still in use among Central Asian nomads. Only some thirty sites are at present known in East Anglia, and all of these are on areas of light soil which would have been open country suitable for grazing. The distribution is of considerable interest. A major concentration occurs at the south end of the Suffolk Sandlings and the adjacent Colchester region of north-east Essex, while a smaller group is found in Breckland and on the Greensand Belt of west Norfolk, with outliers in north Norfolk. When the East Anglian distribution is considered as part of the general British distribution of bell beakers of similar types, and the pottery is compared with continental material, it is clear that the Bell Beaker folk invaded Britain. Their pottery is clearly derived from Holland and the Middle Rhine, and their East Anglian localities indicate the approximate territories seized by these immigrants. In Holland, tanged copper daggers are occasionally found with bell beakers contemporary with our earliest East Anglian specimens, but none of these weapons has so far been found in our area, and in England as a whole less than 5 per cent of beakers of all types have been found with metal objects.

It will be recalled that the widespread and rapid subsidence *c.* 1900 B.C. attested in the Fens, and probably in Broadland, provides a convenient division between Phases II and III of the Neolithic. The Peterborough, Rinyo-Clacton and Bell Beaker cultures survived into the final two centuries of this period from *c.* 1900 B.C. to 1700 B.C., but it would seem that the Windmill Hill culture had died out. Fresh arrivals from overseas and local expansion soon increased the East Anglian population. A few warriors and their followers from Holland or north-western Germany arrived with beakers of corded ware and armed with stone axe-hammers. One of these immigrants was probably responsible for the importation of the axe-hammer found at Langley, Norfolk; this has been examined petrologically, and the material was found to match with rocks from Schleswig-Holstein. Native developments, on the other hand, again characterized by distinctive pottery, are known as the Rusticated Ware and Necked Beaker cultures; though it has been suggested that these are two elements of a common culture. Large vessels of rusticated ware are distinguished by the roughened surface produced by jabbing or by 'pinching', and were probably evolved by descendants of the Mesolithic hunters.

The Necked Beaker culture was, until recently, regarded as an intrusive culture, entirely continental in origin. It now seems

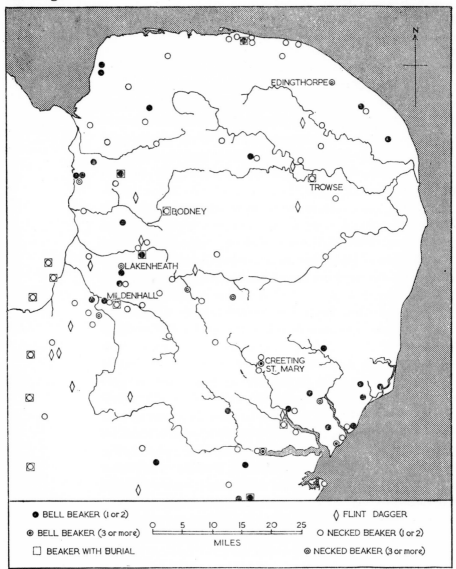

clear, however, that the nucleus of this important culture evolved from the Bell Beaker group already in Britain, though it was influenced to a small extent by the Corded Ware in-vaders. The necked beaker is distinguished by a straight neck rising from a constriction above a globular body. It is profusely decorated with notched stamps and incisions and imprints of reed, bones or finger-nails, sometimes arranged to form triangles, lozenges or saltires. The suggestion that these people used wooden mugs is supported by the form and decoration of handled beakers, large numbers of which were made at Wattisfield, Suffolk, probably during the first phase of the Bronze Age, into which this culture survived. Rusticated ware is often found with necked beaker ware, as are flint dagger blades with fine pressure flaking, barbed and tanged flint arrowheads, perforated stone axe-hammers and polished flint knives—the last probably an East Anglian invention. The main concentration of the Necked Beaker population lies in Breckland, spreading beyond its borders into the Cambridge region, but there is a considerable scatter over the Greensand Belt, the Good Sand region (especially the Cromer-Holt ridge), the Loam region and the Ipswich region, all areas of light soil. These people were nomadic herdsmen, who supple-mented their food supply by fishing and fowling and a little cultivation. Since they had no fixed abodes, they lived in tents which could be easily transported. This conclusion is based on the evidence revealed at Edingthorpe, Norfolk, and Creeting St Mary, Lakenheath and Mildenhall, Suffolk. Here were found numerous hearths, together with pottery, tools and bones of domestic animals, but no indications of permanent buildings. The temporary camp investigated at Lakenheath sprawled over an area of about 120 by 40 yards, suggesting that these herdsmen operated in family groups.

Little is yet known about Necked Beaker burial customs in East Anglia, partly owing to the absence of scientific excavation and partly to the destruction by soil acidity of human remains which may once have been associated with the apparently isolated pots already discovered. It is clear, however, that inhumation was the invariable rite, usually with the body placed in a contracted posture. There the uniformity ends; some bodies were interred beneath round barrows much larger than those of the Bell Beaker culture, while others were placed in isolated graves, apparently unmarked on the surface. Occasionally, as on two sites at Mildenhall, human bones were found scattered in refuse pits, showing a lack of respect for the dead though not necessarily cannibalism. In the centre of a barrow at Trowse, near Norwich, defined by two concentric ditches, were three pits which had been dug for inhumation burials; a necked beaker was associated with one of these.

The varied ancestry of the Late Neolithic population in East Anglia is shown by the physical characteristics of two skeletons buried with necked beakers. At Wherstead, Suffolk, was found the skeleton of a longheaded youth, perhaps descended from the Corded Ware invaders, contrasting with

Plate 11

a broadheaded skeleton with welldeveloped supraorbital ridges found at Bodney, an example of the classical Beaker type, and probably a descendant of one of the Bell Beaker invaders.

Some form of ritual activity must be deduced from the discovery at Bury St Edmunds of sherds of necked beaker and rusticated ware found with pieces of a human skull, which had been charred internally but not cremated. The first recognizable religious centres were constructed during this phase. Two of these hengemonuments, as they are conveniently called, were

Plate 12

discovered by airphotography at Arminghall, near Norwich, and Stratford St Mary in south Suffolk. Only the former has been excavated, revealing the basic elements of its structure, though the nature of the rites performed can only be surmised. The essential feature of these temples is a penannular ditch inside a bank, perhaps used by the congregation, and broken by a single causeway entrance to the central circular sanctuary. At Arminghall, the bank was further defined by a shallow external ditch cut into the sand and gravel. The inner ditch was 28 feet across and had been at least 8 feet deep, while the area it enclosed was 90 feet in diameter. The surrounding bank was 50 feet across at the base, so that the diameter of the whole monument was about 270 feet. In the central area were found holes arranged in horseshoe form for eight gigantic oak posts, $2\frac{1}{2}$ feet to 3 feet in diameter and sunk into the gravel to a depth of $7\frac{1}{2}$ feet. Remains of trees of those dimensions and of similar date are frequently extracted from the fenland peat and their decaying boles can be seen flanking the tracks in Feltwell Fens. It would seem that these posts, the base and sides of which had been charred for preservation, must have stood at least 8 feet above the original ground surface. From the position of the ramps dug to insert them, it is clear that the heavy tree trunks had been dragged downhill to the site from a southerly direction, and had been erected before the inner ditch was dug to obtain material for the bank. At the bottom of the inner ditch, and therefore deriving from the time when the monument was constructed, were found fragments of rusticated ware. The idea that rusticated and necked beaker wares were two products of a common culture is strengthened by the necked beaker discovered in the Trowse barrow, which, with other mounds, forms an integral part of this henge-monument complex. Both these groups have already been described as insular developments, and the idea of henge-monuments, confined to this country, must be part of their native ancestry.

Our survey has now taken us to *c.* 1700 B.C., the terminal date for the Neolithic in East Anglia, with the two counties occupied by people descended from the Mesolithic hunters of an earlier millennium, together with the progeny of various groups of invaders from the continent. Some had lost their separate identity, others had retained distinctive features of pot‑making, burial rite or economic activity. More important even than this variety of cultural groups, is the conversion of East Anglia from a land of hunters to a region of stock‑breeders and farmers.

CHAPTER V

The Bronze Age

METALLURGY, LIKE FARMING, began in the Middle East and its practice spread but slowly into western Europe. Early metal workers soon discovered that by adding one part of tin to nine parts of copper they could produce tools and weapons which were infinitely superior to those of copper alone. This alloy, bronze, was more durable than flint or stone, and the possession of bronze equipment doubtless enhanced the prestige of its owner. Early centres of metal-working were normally situated near accessible deposits of copper ores, as in Ireland where an important centre was established, probably by immigrant Bell Beaker folk, who had been acquainted with the virtues of this metal before they left the Rhineland.

As East Anglia has no native resources of copper or tin, it follows that all the earliest bronze tools must have been imported; indeed, the majority came from Ireland, though some were probably brought from Germany. The introduction of bronze equipment was a slow process, the chieftains being supplied first and their subjects later. Bronze-founding began in East Anglia only when an adequate supply of metal, in the form of obsolete tools, was available in the area to smiths possessing the requisite technical knowledge. For certain specialized purposes, however, flint tools were never entirely superseded throughout the Bronze Age, as flint was readily available over most of the region.

The East Anglian Bronze Age may be divided into two chronological phases, from 1700 to 1100 B.C. and from 1100 to 500 B.C., the first corresponding to the Early and Middle Bronze Ages of other writers and the latter to the Late Bronze Age. Throughout the period, the archaeological evidence comes principally from burials and metal tools, the latter found

Culture	Origin	Phase I	Phase II
		1700 B.C. 1100	500
Necked Beaker	Neolithic survival	———	
Rinyo-Clacton	Neolithic survival	———	
Food-Vessel	From Peterborough culture	———	
	? N. England, ? Wessex		
Wessex	From Wessex	———	
Urn	From Food Vessel culture	———	———
Bucket and Barrel Urn	From Rinyo-Clacton culture		———
Urnfield	From Rinyo-Clacton,		———
	Necked Beaker and Urn		
	cultures		

Chart D   Chart of Bronze Age Cultures

either isolated or in hoards. Owing to the rarity of metal objects associated with burials and to the scarcity of settlement sites, it is often difficult to gain a coherent picture of the daily life of the occupants of the region, or to deduce the interrelations of the varied cultural groups. Some of these had survived with little alteration from the last phase of the Neolithic, the most impor- tant being the Necked Beaker and Rinyo-Clacton cultures, which lasted till *c.* 1500 B.C. and probably later. Handled beakers, which like other beakers may have been used for curds or something stronger, belong to this phase of the Necked Beaker culture. The Food Vessel culture, on the other hand, which was roughly coeval and lasted from *c.* 1700 B.C. to 1400 B.C., is a descendant of the Peterborough culture, though influenced by the Beaker cultures.

The main English concentration of the Food Vessel culture lay in northern England, especially Yorkshire; it takes its name from its typical pottery vase, thick-walled and richly decorated. This type is rare in East Anglia, and it would seem that only a few emigrants from northern England came to settle in Breckland early in Phase I of the local Bronze Age, as is shown by the pottery from Mildenhall and Barton Mills. Other pots assigned to this culture from Needham, Swannington and Wereham in Norfolk, and Pakenham and Icklingham in north-west Suffolk, are rather different from the food vessels of northern England, and these may represent a later distinctive local development. The cremations associated with the food vessels at Needham and Pakenham suggest that these pots are later than the food vessel from Mildenhall. This was buried beneath a round barrow with the contracted body of a broad-headed female under a heap of eighteen red deer antlers, which were presumably an offering. Other contracted inhumations found without grave-goods beneath round bowl barrows, probably also belong to the early phase of this culture.

Plate 13

The relatively few pottery food vessels so far recorded from East Anglia may be due to the more common use of wooden vessels, which were perhaps normally interred with the dead; even so, the limited number of burials associated with this culture suggests that its members formed only a small group. In addition to their characteristic pottery, other items of equipment point to their presence—the widely distributed small pressure-flaked flint knives, plano-convex in shape, as well as the rarer jet beads, probably brought from the Whitby area. A jet necklace was found with a copper awl on the skeleton of a young woman at Methwold ('Southery') who had most likely been drowned, and odd beads have been found elsewhere. Necklaces of bone, made possibly from the ribs of red deer and obviously copies of jet beads, have been discovered at Feltwell, Norfolk, and with a cremation in a barrow at Barton Mills, Suffolk. In the north of England some Food Vessel people were buried in rough tree-trunk coffins, and it is probable that a coffin discovered in 1720 in a marsh at West Tofts in south-west Norfolk belongs to this culture. With this skeleton were jet and gold objects and 'blue beads', possibly of faience, the origin of which will be discussed later. It would appear from the distribution of the above sites that the main activities of the local Food Vessel folk were confined to Norfolk and north-west Suffolk, where they roamed with their herds, pausing at times to sow and reap a corn crop.

These people probably also acted as traders, continuing the Peterborough tradition. They were probably responsible for the very few early metal tools which reached the less wealthy inhabitants of the heathlands in the Ipswich area, the Necked Beaker and Rinyo-Clacton people who still survived with their Neolithic equipment. Imported bronzes are scattered over the lighter soils of Norfolk but are more common in Breckland and the adjacent Cambridge region, where they were used princi-pally by the Food Vessel people. The chief metal type brought to East Anglia from Ireland at this time was the thick-butted flat axehead, but a few halberds—hafted weapons with dagger-like blades at right angles—awls and flat knife-daggers have also been recorded. Trade with Scandinavia is indicated by several flint dagger blades of distinctive type found in Breckland. These commercial contacts will be further emphasized when we consider the luxurious equipment of the Wessex culture people, whose activities must now engage our attention.[1]

Wessex lay astride the main trade routes from Ireland to the continent, and about 1550 B.C. its chieftains began to grow wealthy through the profits of this international commerce. An 'heroic' society of warrior-chieftains can be recognized from numerous rich and elaborate interments in distinctive burial mounds. The reconstruction of Stonehenge epitomizes the power and wealth of one of the monarchs of this Wessex culture, which lasted in full vigour for about two centuries. During that time, the luxurious tastes of these pastoralists and traders were satisfied by imports from Ireland, South Germany,

Fig. 16 Flat bronze axehead. Harding-ham, Norfolk. Scale ½

[1] See also *Wessex* by J. F. S. Stone, No. 9 in the 'Ancient Peoples and Places' series, London, 1958.

Bohemia, Scandinavia, Greece and Egypt. From Ireland came bronze axes with cast flanges, awls, daggers with mid-ribs or grooves, and ornaments of sheet gold; from Northern Europe came the inspiration for the stone battle-axes and the amber for ornaments, which was received through Central Europe, from whence came distinctive bronze pins. The blue, segmented faience beads were made mainly in Egypt where they can be dated to *c.* 1400 B.C., and it seems probable that they reached these shores through the agency of Mycenean seafarers.

The Wessex chieftains held sway over Wiltshire, Dorset and adjacent parts of Berkshire, Hampshire and Somerset, but some of them ventured farther afield. A group of these warlike herds-men moved up the Icknield Way into west Norfolk, where they presumably formed a ruling class over the Food Vessel people already there, and later over their descendants, the Urn Folk. Like other pastoralists, the Wessex overlords had no fixed abode, and the burial mounds of their distinguished dead are their principal monuments. Their barrows are normally sur-rounded by a ditch with an external bank, and two main types —the bell and disc barrow—may be distinguished. The bell barrow has a high, round mound with a narrow berm separating it from the ditch, the whole being sometimes as much as 180 feet in diameter. This type can be recognized in *Fig. 17* groups of barrows at Rushford in Breckland and at Great Bircham, West Rudham and Weasenham in the Good Sand region. The disc barrow consists of a small mound in the centre of a flat circular area bounded by ditch and bank, and is easily obliterated by ploughing. Barrows of this type have been identified at Wellingham, forming part of the Weasenham group, at Rushford and Salthouse in west and north Norfolk, and at Martlesham in the Sandlings of south-east Suffolk. Bell barrows usually contain male cremations or inhumations, while disc barrows were erected over cremated females, the latter rite being probably derived from the Secondary Neolithic cultures

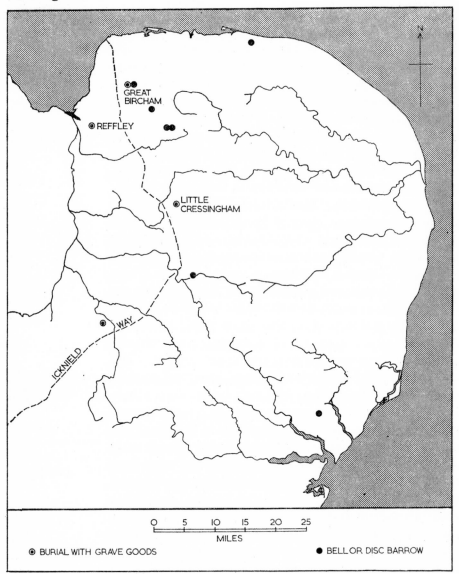

Fig. 17   Distribution of Wessex culture in East Anglia

of Wessex. In a bell barrow at Great Bircham was found a cairn of flints covering an inverted urn with loop handles con⁄ taining cremated bones, a bronze awl and gold⁄covered beads, apparently the possessions of a chieftain's wife. The contracted body of a male found at Little Cressingham was presumably buried fully clothed, with his grooved bronze dagger with a wooden hilt, a flat bronze dagger, a necklace of amber beads and pendants, a thin rectangular gold plate and other sheet gold mountings. This burial, dating from *c.* 1500 B.C., indicates a very early expansion of the Wessex culture into Norfolk. Some of the other barrows surviving at Little Cressingham, though not of distinctive Wessex types, may also mark inter⁄ ments of the same group. Another Wessex chieftain of slightly later date has been found interred under a round barrow at Chippenham, Cambridgeshire, with a grooved dagger and a perforated axe⁄hammer of picrite, a rock native to Mont⁄ gomeryshire. Traders thus brought to East Anglia bronze and gold from Ireland, amber from the Baltic and stone from the Welsh border, and some of the blue glazed faience beads from Egypt. The Wessex chieftains were probably responsible for the vogue of these attractive objects among their subjects. These beads have been found at Sutton Hoo and Lakenheath, Suffolk, and at Reffley on the outskirts of King's Lynn, where a ring⁄ pendant, also of this material, was found in a round barrow with cremations and overhanging⁄rim urns of the Urn Folk. From Rockland All Saints, Norfolk, comes a stone mace or sceptre head, probably the symbol of authority of some petty chieftain, imitating the wood, shale and gold⁄mounted sceptres of the Wessex princelings.

By *c.* 1400 B.C. the material culture of the Food Vessel people had evolved, and from this date onwards it can be described as the Urn culture, which persisted until the end of the Bronze Age in Norfolk and north⁄west Suffolk. This culture is recognized by the large ill⁄fired, hand⁄made urns of coarse clay,

Plate 14

Fig. 18 Segmented faience bead. Reffley, King's Lynn, Nor⁄ folk. Actual size

75

Fig. 19   Overhanging-rim urn from barrow, Witton, north-east Norfolk. Height 18 in.

Fig. 19

fabricated by its women-folk and known to us chiefly as receptacles for the cremated remains of the dead. One type, which may be regarded as an unusually tall version of the food vessel, is distinguished by an overhanging-rim, and is commonly decorated with twisted cord impressions. Another type is plain and biconical, while yet others are decorated in relief with finger-tip ornament, probably derived from the Rinyo-Clacton culture. These various types of urn were once placed in a chronological sequence, but it now seems likely that they are all roughly contemporaneous in their first appearance and reflect the diverse traditions of their makers' ancestry.

Few settlements of the Urn Folk have been recognized, pottery such as that from Edingthorpe, Norfolk, and Mildenhall, Suffolk, being the only evidence of domestic occupation. The poor quality of their pottery is inimical to its survival, but the rarity of settlement sites is mainly due to their way of life. Like their forbears, the Urn Folk were primarily nomadic pastoralists, whose most permanent shelter may have been a round skin tent. The products of their flocks were supplemented by hunting, and occasionally by hoe-agriculture, when they cultivated barley and wheat.

These nomadic people are thus known to us almost entirely from the contents of the round barrows they erected or enlarged to contain the cremated remains of their dead. This rite became common in northern East Anglia *c.* 1400 B.C., and was universal a couple of centuries later. The large quantities of fuel needed for this practice must have depleted the woodlands on the lighter soils, and thus expanded the area available for the pasturing of flocks. Of the few East Anglian round barrows which have been adequately explored, fewer still have been published, so that little is yet known about the probably elaborate ritual accompanying all stages of the cremation cere-mony and construction of the barrow. If death occurred when a group of these herdsmen was far from their traditional burial ground, grazing their flocks, a mound may have been con-structed close by or the body smoke-dried and carried round on a shaggy pony until the nomads again came near their own barrow group, often situated near a well-used trackway. Once the funeral pyre was burnt out, the cremated bones would be placed in a cinerary urn or in a leather or cloth bag, secured by a bronze pin. This would be inserted in a hole dug in an existing barrow, or a fresh barrow would be constructed by scraping up the surrounding topsoil or by digging, thus forming an encircling ditch. The urn would often be inverted beneath a small heap of flints, or placed under a cairn of turf capped by sand or clay. The barrow was sometimes revetted with chalk, and thus, when freshly constructed, must have been a con∕ spicuous landmark. Most of the barrows in East Anglia are isolated, but rows of three or four are not uncommon and even larger cemeteries are known, such as the thirty barrows on Brightwell and Martlesham Heaths in Suffolk, perhaps erected over several generations.

Fig. 20

About two hundred and fifty round barrows now survive or are known to have existed in Norfolk, and about one hundred in Suffolk, but the original numbers must have been consider∕ ably larger, for many mounds have been flattened by ploughing, so that only circular marks in an arable field remain. Not all the barrows shown on the map were necessarily erected or even used by the Urn Folk, but this probably applies to the majority, and their distribution indicates the extent of the area roamed over by groups of these herdsmen. Many earlier barrows

Fig. 21

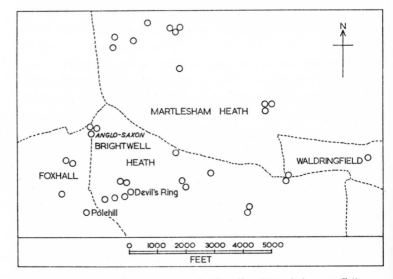

Fig. 20   Bronze Age barrow group at Brightwell and Martlesham, Suffolk

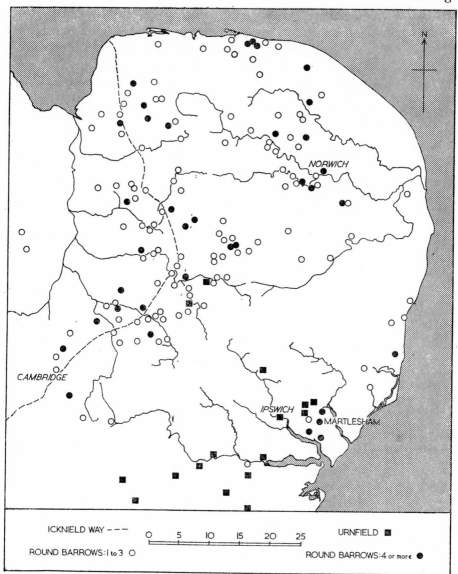

Fig. 21   Distribution of round barrows and Late Bronze Age urnfields

were rebuilt and enlarged by the Urn Folk to contain the remains of an increasing population, as at Witton, near North
Walsham, where a ditch-encircled barrow, with an original
inhumation burial, had been enlarged by the Urn Folk and a
second, wider, ditch dug, so that seven cremations could be
inserted in the enlarged mound which now covered the earlier
ditch. These burial mounds should, therefore, be regarded as
small cemeteries. The Urn Folk may occasionally have interred
the cremated bones in flat cemeteries, but these have not been
adequately investigated and may be the remains of barrows from
which the mounds have been removed. The distribution of
barrows of the Urn Folk shows that their herds grazed most of
the lighter soils of Norfolk and north-west Suffolk, while the
dense woodland of High Suffolk separated them from their
kinsmen who roamed the heathlands of the Sandlings. It may
well have been the pressure of an expanding population that
caused some of the Urn Folk, between *c.* 1400 and 1200 B.C.,
to take boat and migrate from this coastal area to Holland, an
unusual reversal of one of the fundamental trends in East
Anglian archaeology.

Our picture of the possessions of the Urn Folk is necessarily
restricted to those objects which have been placed with the
cremated bones after the funeral ceremony, and to the rare
occupation debris. An example of the influence of the Wessex
chieftains may be seen in the association of small pots (pygmy
vessels) with cinerary urns. Bronze awls, shale rings, stone axe-
hammers and animal bones have also been found in East
Anglian barrows of the Urn culture. The evidence for the
development of a local bronze industry *c.* 1200 B.C. can be
inferred from hoards or caches of weapons and tools deliberately
buried in the ground and never recovered by their owners.
These may consist of the personal possessions of one individual,
such as the rapier, axe and sickle found in the fen at Downham
Market, Norfolk, or the stock-in-trade of an itinerant metal-

Fig. 22

Plate 15

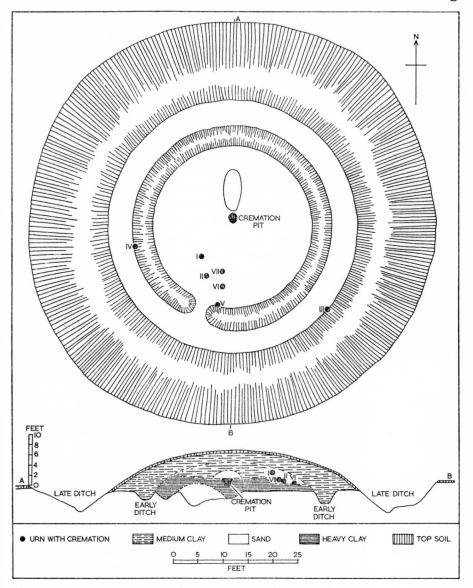

Fig. 22   Plan and section of round barrow at Witton, north-east Norfolk

smith, such as the group of seventy axes and spearheads found at Stibbard, in the same county. The axes in this hoard had been concealed unfinished, for their edges had not been sharpened for use. Metalsmiths probably served all sections of the community, and may well have formed a distinctive social group. They derived the bulk of their raw material from melting, down obsolete tools, and cast fresh tools and weapons according to the needs of their customers. In addition to the awls, rapiers and axes ('palstaves') already mentioned, the chief products were daggers, spearheads with loops at the base of the blade for securing to the haft, and axes with cast flanges.

There are many difficulties in the interpretation of the archaeological material of Phase II of the Bronze Age, which lasted from *c*. 1100 B.C. to *c*. 500 B.C. These will remain until more settlement sites have been discovered, where pottery, at present largely known from burials, may be found associated with bronze implements. In the past, hypothetical invasions have been conjured up to explain some of the novel features of this phase, and cultural labels have been employed which have only obscured the real problems. A considerable expansion of the bronze/founding industry, with the introduction of many new types of tools and weapons, and the widespread adoption of cremated burial in flat cemeteries can be recognized in south/east England generally. But East Anglia lay on the fringe of these developments and over most of its area there was a sturdy survival of earlier tradition.

In Norfolk and north/west Suffolk few burials of this phase of the Bronze Age are known. Plain biconical urns from barrows probably of this date show that the Urn Folk were still building burial mounds or enlarging those of their ancestors. Often, however, they were still merely inserting a bag of cremated bones into the side of an earlier barrow. Some cinerary urns, similar to those from barrows, have been found without any trace of an accompanying mound at Rockland St Andrew

Plate 21

and Needham, Norfolk, indicating that the custom of barrow burial was obsolete among some groups. Its persistence else/where, probably into the closing years of Phase II of the Bronze Age, is shown by the construction on Salthouse Heath, Norfolk, adjacent to the earlier barrow cemetery built by the Beaker Folk and Urn Folk, of tiny mounds only a few feet in diameter, each with a centrally placed bucket/shaped urn con/ taining cremated bones. The evidence of burials suggests, therefore, that groups of the Urn Folk, each with its own practices, remained for six centuries as the principal inhabitants of Norfolk and north/west Suffolk, until *c.* 500 B.C. Yet there were other elements in the local population during this phase whose origins are not easy to explain.

The small community which had dwelt on the edge of Mildenhall Fen in Phase I and used overhanging/rim urns and cord/impressed pottery, was succeeded in Phase II by a family group which made its pots in the shape of buckets, barrels and bags. When decorated, these vessels were ornamented by impressing the finger/nail or finger/tip round the rim or widest part of the body. This pottery can scarcely have evolved from that of the Urn Folk; it may represent an intrusion from southern England, but more probably was produced locally by descendants of the old Neolithic Rinyo/Clacton culture. This was thought to have ended *c.* 1500 B.C., but the first of these bucket and barrel urns is unlikely to be earlier than *c.* 1100 B.C., so that an awkward gap of four hundred years has to be bridged if this hypothesis is correct. In this case, we must assume a survival in northern East Anglia of Rinyo/Clacton people alongside the Urn Folk; we shall see that something similar may well have happened in the Ipswich region.

Before considering the evidence from the Ipswich region, further attention must be given to the economy and dwelling sites of these Bucket and Barrel Urn people. The site in Mildenhall Fen, already mentioned, was clearly occupied by farmers who kept sheep, goats and oxen, herded with the help of dogs, and who also, from the evidence of flint saddle-querns, consumed cereals. The survival of earlier traditions is shown by the hunting of red and roe deer, the trapping of otters and by the production of flint tools of clumsy technique. A bronze saw-blade and tweezers found close to a similar, but later, settlement at Grime's Graves, probably dating from the seventh or sixth century B.C., shows that these people were equipped with metal implements. We may assume the cultivation of flax or nettles from the survival of a thread of linen in a bronze hoard found at Somerleyton, Suffolk, the earliest textile so far recorded from the area, and domestic weaving is attested by the discovery of cylindrical clay loom weights at, for instance, Heacham in Norfolk.

Settlement sites of a different character are suggested by ill-recorded discoveries made during the last century in some of the Breckland meres, when these were temporarily drained for farming purposes. In West Mere, West Wretham, a circular mound of sand was exposed, linked by a wall of flint and marl to a well fenced with alder stakes and wattling. The bones of numerous animals, mainly oxen, killed by an axe-blow on the skull, lay near by. In Mickle Mere, in the same parish, an artificial island and a structure of oak piles were reported, as well as a large dump of the bones and horns of deer, ox and pig and part of a bronze axe. In Barton Mere, Pakenham, Suffolk, a small oval structure of wattles was excavated and several bronze spearheads were found. Somewhat similar finds have also been recorded from other natural lakes in East Anglia. The objects found have almost all been lost, but it seems clear that these constructions were made in the Bronze Age when the water level was lower. There are no exotic bronze implements to link these activities with the arrival of emigrants from the Alpine area, who in other parts of Britain erected pile dwellings along rivers, or crannogs in marshes. It is unfortunate that the pottery

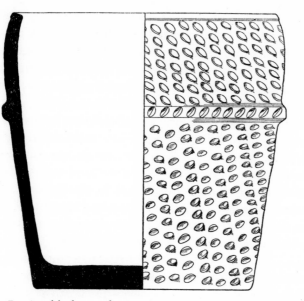

Fig. 23   Rusticated bucket urn from urnfield. Ipswich, Suffolk. Height 13¼ in.

from these sites was not preserved, leaving us in doubt as to whether the Urn Folk or the Bucket and Barrel Urn makers were responsible. It would seem that those who built these structures were attracted by the water-supply and by the fishing, and probably dwelt by the water's edge after they had butchered most of their beasts in the autumn. Further exploration is clearly required, as is a search in fen areas for brushwood causeways similar to those of Late Bronze Age date already recognized in the Cambridgeshire Fens.

During Phase II there is a remarkable contrast between the burial customs in the Ipswich-Colchester region and those in the rest of East Anglia. The custom of barrow burial, wide-spread in Phase I among the Urn Folk who lived in the sandy heathlands of the Ipswich area, was replaced in Phase II by the practice of 'urnfield' burial. These urnfields or 'flat cemeteries' contained groups of urns unmarked by mounds, in which had been placed the cremated remains of the dead, with occasional flint flakes as the only associated objects. At least eight of these cemeteries have been discovered near Ipswich, the more impor⁄ tant being at Little Bealings, Playford, Rushmere, Nayland and Brantham. At two sites in Breckland—Honington and Knettishall—something similar has also been recorded, and it is possible that these may form an outlier of the Ipswich⁄ Colchester group. Although none has been excavated in its entirety, several of these flat cemeteries have each yielded over twenty urns, and one as many as a hundred. These urns are mainly of barrel or bucket shape, similar in form to those from Breckland already mentioned, but they also include some biconical vessels; usually all are plain, but when decorated bear applied bands with finger⁄tip or finger⁄nail impressions below the rim or over the body. Urns from at least five cemeteries have *Fig. 23* the whole body covered with finger⁄printing ('rustication'), a distinctive feature almost confined to this area.

These cemeteries exhibit some interesting features and pose some difficult problems. The adoption of urnfield burial and the cessation of the practice of providing the deceased with possessions for the underworld imply innovations in religious belief. The size of the cemeteries suggests use over several centuries, or, more probably, that the population was now larger than in previous periods. The presence of a denser population points to a more settled economy than the nomadic pastoralism of the earlier Urn Folk. These cemeteries are situated not only on the sandy heathlands around Ipswich, but also on the richer soils of the Colchester Loam area and the Boulder Clay Plateau of north Essex, which could have been tilled with the aid of a light plough, now available for the first time. This increase in the density and area of distribution of the population would only have been possible if settled mixed farming had replaced nomadic pastoralism.

Previously, it has been held that these revolutionary innovations must indicate an invasion from the Low Countries,
where somewhat similar pottery is known. The distribution of
the East Anglian cemeteries would favour the notion of sea-
borne invaders disembarking in the estuaries of the Orwell,
Stour or Colne, and indeed invasion from the continent in the
Late Bronze Age is well established, as in the case of north
French refugees in Kent. But the pottery of the Low Countries
can no longer be regarded as ancestral to the East Anglian
cremation urns, for the former had evolved from the pottery of
British emigrants who left our shores for the Netherlands in
Phase I, as mentioned above. If we may no longer look abroad
for a solution to this problem, we must consider whether the
occupants of our urnfields could have migrated from any other
part of Britain. Though this is feasible, it is unlikely, for some
of the types of urn, such as the 'rusticated' vessels, are not really
matched elsewhere. We are therefore driven to the conclusion
that the origins of this group must be sought in the immediate
vicinity, and, despite the chronological gap, that this Urnfield
culture, with its bucket, barrel and biconical urns, resulted from
the fusion of the traditions of the Rinyo-Clacton culture,
Necked Beaker culture (with its large rusticated pots) and Urn
culture, a conclusion strengthened by the form or decoration of
its pottery, which reveals the influence of one or more of these
earlier groups.

One of the striking features of Phase II of the East Anglian
Bronze Age is that its cultural development took place locally
without foreign influence. Certain items of the bronze equipment are undoubtedly foreign in derivation, due to the arrival
in Britain of alien smiths, but some tools and weapons show the
continuity of native tradition. The increase in the production
and use of bronze equipment during Phase II is remarkable,
the surviving objects being roughly ten times as numerous
as those from the preceding phase, though this disparity is

accentuated by the melting-down of earlier equipment for use in the later phase. Most of the bronzes have been recovered from hoards concealed by itinerant metal-founders during their peregrinations from one group of customers to another; at least forty have been recorded from East Anglia. These caches, comprising obsolete and broken tools ready for melting down, lumps of metal cake and newly cast and often unfinished tools and weapons—sometimes over a hundred objects in all—are frequently found isolated from any known settlement sites or burial places, though this isolation may be more apparent than real. Some hoards, as at Norgate Road, Norwich, and at Butley, Suffolk, were obviously buried near the site of a tem-porary smithy, as the debris of metalworking has been found

Plate 16

scattered over a wide area; but only rarely, as in the Unthank Road hoard, Norwich, has a bronze mould for casting been found. The siting of these temporary smithies was influenced by two main factors: it was essential that there should be an adequate wood supply for the production of charcoal, and that the smithy should be located near routes normally used by the potential customers. It is possible that herdsmen and farmers congregated at certain seasons for religious ceremonies, occasions which would also facilitate trade.

Continental craftsmen were probably responsible, between *c.* 1000 and 800 B.C., for the principal additions to the arma-ment of the local chieftains and their retinues. The most common weapons found are socketed axeheads, slashing swords with leaf-shaped blades and rounded shoulders, and spearheads which were secured to the haft by pegs. British metalsmiths soon copied these types, or modified weapons like their traditional rapier to imitate the new and superior sword, as is apparent from an unfinished example found at Caistor-by-Norwich. Palstaves and looped spearheads continued to be made with various modifications. Objects of adornment were also fashioned, such as the torcs, bracelets, finger rings and large quoit-headed pins found in a hoard at Barton Bendish, Norfolk; a disc-headed pin from Lakenheath is perhaps a native copy of a north European type.

From *c.* 800 B.C. onwards many continental types of weapon were being imported to the Lower Thames, Essex and Hertfordshire, or made there by foreign metalsmiths. The most distinctive of these were the carp's-tongue type of thrusting-sword with its bag-shaped chape, derived from western France, and the winged bronze axehead of west Alpine inspiration. Some of the new equipment found its way northwards into East Anglia to become incorporated in the stock-in-trade of local smiths. Carp's-tongue sword fragments occurred in a hoard at Gorleston, Great Yarmouth, a characteristic chape comes from a hoard at Felixstowe, and winged axes have been found in hoards at Carleton Rode, Norfolk, and Butley and Somerleyton, Suffolk. Local imitations of these axes, with the wings cast as decoration, have been noted at Norwich, Ipswich and Lakenheath.

Native smiths in East Anglia during the next two centuries (800–600 B.C.) were producing socketed axeheads in large quantities, making two-edged socketed knives and slashing swords with straight shoulders, and hammering-out sheet metal to make magnificent circular shields of the type recovered from Sutton, Norfolk. The smiths made socketed bronze sickles for the farmer, saws, chisels and gouges for the car-penter, who in his turn constructed wooden containers and dug-out boats for river transport.

Though the bulk of the equipment required by the herds-men and arable farmers of East Anglia was produced locally, imports from many lands were needed for the total satisfaction of their demands. Socketed axeheads of a type commonly found in Yorkshire were probably brought to our region by sea, and others from South Wales were traded up the Icknield Way. From farther afield, square-mouthed Breton axes reached

Plate 18

Plate 19

Plate 17

the Cambridge region and adjacent parts of Breckland, while 'indented socketed axes', found at Frettenham and Oxwick, Norfolk, are probably also of French origin. Metalworkers in Ireland were still as skilful as ever in the production of gold and bronze work; a hoard of four Irish gold bracelets and cloak-fasteners found at Caister-by-Yarmouth (though perhaps buried there at a later date) may indicate an export route to the continent in the seventh century B.C. The discovery of similar gold cloak-fasteners elsewhere in Norfolk shows that these luxury articles were also worn locally. Not all gold objects, however, came from Ireland, for the decoration on two gold collars from Geldeston, Norfolk, suggests a north German origin. A further product of Irish inspiration is a bronze cauldron found at Ipswich, probably dating from the last century of the Bronze Age (600–500 B.C.).

To this last century of the Bronze Age must also be attributed the winged chapes of sword scabbards found at Lakenheath. These and other continental bronzes, scattered south from East Anglia to the Thames, are relics of 'tip and run' raids by small groups of warriors using Belgium as a base, and forming a prelude to the Iron Age settlement which, on parts of the East Coast, began before 500 B.C.

We must not allow the wealth of metal equipment from the second phase of the Bronze Age to eclipse the importance of the development of well-balanced mixed farming and a more settled population out of the predominantly pastoral economy of the Urn Folk. The hoe had now been superseded by the light plough which enabled farmers to cultivate the heavier but more fertile loams, thus increasing the yield of cereal crops, especially barley. The more systematic herding of cattle and grazing of sheep, attested in southern England, must have improved the stock. The harnessing of draught ponies to wheeled vehicles in the seventh century B.C. was a further contribution to this agricultural revolution.

CHAPTER VI

The Iron Age

I N THE LAST CHAPTER we have noted that raiders, based on Belgium, harassed the East Coast during the sixth century B.C. About 500 B.C., peasant farmers, driven by the mounting pressure of migrating tribes, came to East Anglia from southern Holland, and central and eastern Belgium. These displaced persons brought with them a knowledge of iron, the use of which had been general in central Europe for some three centuries. The arrival in England of these Iron Age A people opened the first phase of the Iron Age, which lasted till *c.* 300 B.C. The acid soils of East Anglia, together with the colder and wetter climatic conditions of this period, have led to the destruction of iron equipment of this date, but its former presence is suggested by the marks of metal tools on bone and antler; bronze tools would have survived, but the total absence of metal equipment from most sites of this period suggests that iron must have been the metal employed. Iron is more easily worked and more effective than bronze, while the wider diffusion of iron ores enabled weapons and agricultural implements to be produced cheaply. The gravel and greensand deposits of East Anglia contain much low-grade iron ore, but there is at present no evidence that these were exploited on a large scale before the Roman period. In the absence of surviving iron equipment—less than a dozen iron objects are known from the whole of the Iron Age in our area—the presence of Iron Age A immigrants is chiefly indicated by their domestic pottery, mainly jars and bowls of both coarse and fine fabric, which are found together even on the earliest sites. There is a wide variety of shape from the highly angular to the rounded profile, and most of these vessels are undecorated. Much of the finer-textured pottery was coated with a fine slip, sometimes of

Culture	Origin	Phase I 500 B.C. 300	Phase II 150	Phase III A.D. 43
Urn and Urnfield	Bronze Age survival	———		
Iron Age A	Low Countries			
Iron Age B	France		———	———
(Marnians)				
Iron Age C	France and Belgium			———
(Belgae)	via S.E. England			

Chart E   *Chart of Iron Age Cultures*

haematite, before burnishing. Some vessels in the coarse fabric, which is heavily gritted with flint, were decorated at the rim or shoulder with finger-tip impressions or diagonal cuts or stabs.

Variations in pottery form and decoration establish that this invasion was a gradual infiltration of family groups or small clans. Sometimes they settled down peaceably alongside Bronze Age farmers, as at Snettisham, Norfolk; other settlers selected sites some distance from any known Late Bronze Age farms, as at West Harling, where the plan of the round houses indicates the peaceful absorption of native architectural ideas. These Iron Age A immigrants increased to form the most numerous element of the East Anglian population during the rest of the Iron Age and the Roman period. Throughout Phase I of the Iron Age, as in earlier periods, there is a contrast between the cultures of the populations of the Breckland and Ipswich regions. The invaders from the Low Countries who settled in Breckland are clearly related to communities round the Fenland basin in Cambridgeshire and Northamptonshire, though the Fenland itself was uninhabitable owing to a minor rise in sea-level. The settlers in the Ipswich region, related to those in the Colchester Loam area and in the Lower Thames area, came from other parts of the Low Countries. There was also sporadic settlement along the north Norfolk coast, shown by finds at

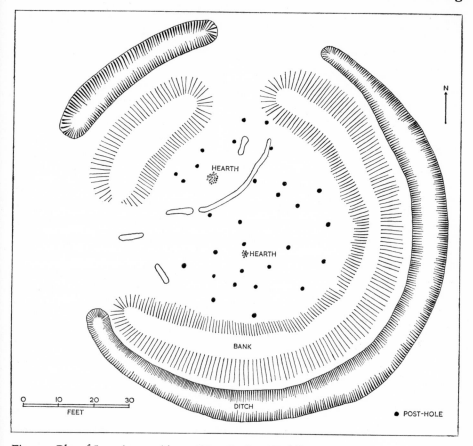

N

HEARTH

HEARTH

BANK

DITCH

O   10   20   30
FEET

● POST-HOLE

Fig. 24   Plan of Iron Age round house. West Harling, Norfolk

Plate 20

Stiffkey, at Cromer and at Paston, and in the forested area of north Suffolk, where clay for potting may have been the attraction. It seems probable that outside these areas the Late Bronze Age population continued, for a century or so, to use some of the bronze equipment attributed to Phase II of the Bronze Age.

The chief surviving features of farmsteads of the first phase of the Iron Age are ditches, pits or post-holes, but at only one East Anglian site, West Harling, has the overall plan been revealed. The West Harling farmstead lies on a glacial knoll, Micklemoor Hill, adjacent to the River Thet. The structures identified comprise a circular Eastern Enclosure with a turf bank (72 feet in diameter) surrounded by an external drainage ditch, an oval Western Enclosure (94 by 106 feet) with bank and shallow ditch, and a fragmentary Southern Enclosure of rectangular plan, again with shallow ditches. Within the

Fig. 24

Eastern Enclosure, which had two causeway-entrances, were two concentric penannular settings of holes for oak posts, which formed the framework of a round house with a porch facing north. Hearths of crackled flints, hollows of various shapes which may have been for cooking, and runnels, were also detected. It is likely that the bank was an integral part of the house and the complete roofing of such a large area would present many problems. It would seem more likely that the

Fig. 25

house was penannular in plan, with an entrance on the west to an internal circular yard; the ridge-roof of the house drained into this and into the external ditch which also served as a refuse dump. A circular setting of post-holes was found in the middle of the Western Enclosure, and this somewhat smaller house may have had a conical roof. Inside the Southern Enclosure were traces of a rectangular building, at least 27 feet long and constructed with sleeper beams into which round vertical posts may have been set. The rectangular plan of this building may have been an innovation introduced by its foreign builders. These farmers herded oxen and sheep and, in addition, cultivated cereals, as is indicated by an impression of wheat (probably spelt) on a potsherd and by saddle-querns for grinding grain. They hunted wild pig, red deer, the crane and the beaver, probably with the help of a dog—whose bones were found. During the occupation of this farmstead (probably not more than one or two generations) flint tools were knapped by the menfolk, while their wives and daughters made the domestic crockery—the remains of at least five hundred and thirty pots were thrown into the ditch round the Eastern house—and spun yarn, as is shown by the discovery of clay spindle-whorls. Domestic weaving on a vertical loom is suggested by the sur-vival of triangular clay loom weights at other farmsteads. Unlike many Iron Age A farmers between Cambridgeshire and the South Coast, the East Anglian farmers of this culture do not appear to have dug pits for grain storage, possibly using instead large jars; though a group of deep pits at Darmsden in Barking

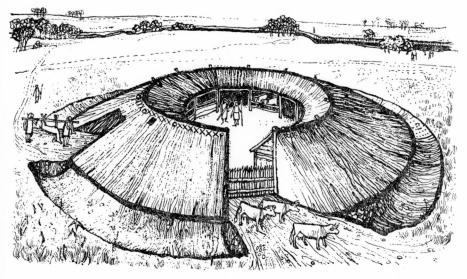

Fig. 25   Reconstruction of Iron Age round house. West Harling, Norfolk

parish, Suffolk, may represent an exception. The keeping qualities of the grain were enhanced by parching in clay ovens before storage; the remains of such an oven have been found at Stutton, Suffolk. No traces of Iron Age fields have been recognized in East Anglia, doubtless due to later destruction.

Little is known of the burial customs of these farmers between 500 and 300 B.C., and both inhumation and cremation may have been the custom. Iron Age A pottery has been found in barrows at Stiffkey and Weeting, Norfolk, but the former contained no human remains, while the pottery from the latter may not be associated with the cremated bones, and it is not even certain if the barrows are of the same age as the pottery. In another burial mound at Barrow, Suffolk, two iron spear heads imitating Bronze Age types were discovered, but here too the burial rite is unknown.

The apparent poverty of these Iron Age A peasant farmers of Phase I is most marked, while the virtual absence of iron equipment prevents us from assessing the skill of the local black smiths. None of the farmsteads has yet yielded any significant ornaments, but a few bronze safety pins for fastening garments are recorded as coming from Felixstowe, Icklingham, Ixworth and Lakenheath in Suffolk. None of these has, however, been recovered by excavation and their associations are unknown; if they are genuine local finds, they must be regarded as fifth century imports from the Alpine region or northern Italy. Other alleged imports include a fragmentary bronze bowl with re peating horse design, paralleled in Austria, and a leaf shaped bronze brooch of Scandinavian type, also reputed to come from Ixworth or its vicinity.

By *c.* 300 B.C. the pottery of the Iron Age A farmers had evolved, with the profile becoming less angular, the rim more rounded and the surface smoother; many of these types survived almost unchanged in form and fabric until the very end of the Iron Age. It is difficult from the evidence of pottery alone to distinguish the farmsteads of Phase II (300–150 B.C.) from those of Phase III. Some earlier sites continued to be occupied, but many fresh farms were established during this phase, in/cluding some by immigrants from Wessex. Few structural details are known, but from the evidence of air photographs it may be assumed that round houses of the West Harling type predominated, though rectangular buildings were also being erected, such as the huts excavated at Rickinghall Inferior, Suffolk, and at Snarehill, Norfolk. Only too often a hearth of fired flints, a group of refuse pits, potsherds or animal bones is all that remains to indicate the site of a flourishing farm. Equally little is known of the agricultural economy of East Anglia at this time, but evidence from other areas of southern England indicates that sheep grazing had greatly increased, probably on the wide tracts of rough grassland on the lighter soils. Wheat is usually regarded as the dominant cereal crop of the Iron Age in Britain, but six/row barley has been recorded from Thriplow, Cambridgeshire, and both crops may have been grown in East Anglia at this time.

Both cremation and inhumation were practised in Phase II. Cremated human bones have been found in jars at Creeting St Mary and Lakenheath, Suffolk, while the skeletons of a long/headed woman and her child were found with potsherds and animal bones in a refuse pit at Roudham in Breckland. Dis/memberment before burial, or the disturbance of earlier graves, seems indicated by the discovery of fragmentary human skeletal remains in refuse pits at Heacham, Norfolk.

The peaceful development of this peasant society of the Iron Age A culture, engaged in tilling small plots, pasturing sheep, oxen and horses, was rudely shattered in the middle of the third century B.C. by the arrival of aristocratic warriors and their retainers, hailing from the Marne region of France, who introduced to eastern Britain the first of our Iron Age B cultures. These people, known to archaeologists as Marnians, raided

Fig. 26

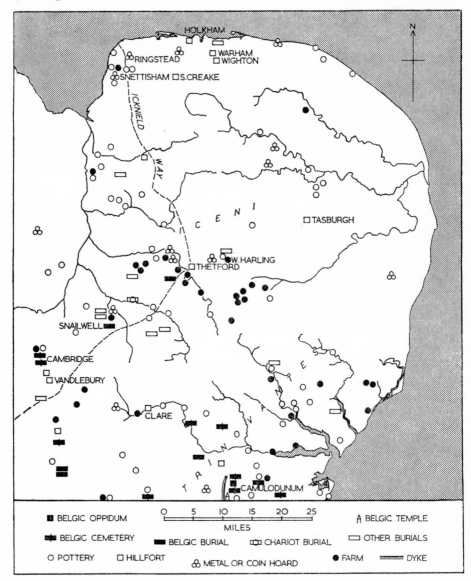

Fig. 26 *Distribution of Iron Age cultures*

East Anglia probably along the rivers leading inland from the Wash, or overland from the Thames estuary. An imported iron sword in a decorated bronze scabbard found near Wisbech, Cambridgeshire, is a relic of one of these mid⁄third⁄century raids. Local chieftains, alarmed by these incursions, erected fortifications which would have been defended by the subject peasantry around. Fifteen acres of the hilltop of Vandlebury, on the Gog Magog Hills outside Cambridge, were enclosed with a circular ditch and timber⁄revetted rampart at about this time to protect the farmstead of a chieftain. It is possible that the enclosures at Narborough, Tasburgh and South Creake in Norfolk, fortified by a single rampart and ditch and loosely termed 'hillforts', resulted from fear of attack on the part of other Iron Age chieftains. By the end of the third century some of these Marnians had established themselves around the margins of Fenland, presumably becoming suzerains of the Iron Age A population. Fresh reinforcements from France continued to arrive during the second century, as is shown by the dagger in a delicate bronze sheath from 'Hertford Warren', a locality believed to be near Bury St Edmunds.

Plate 22

The success of the Marnians was due to their military prowess and to the superiority of their equipment, for they introduced chariot warfare to Britain, as devastating an innovation as that of the tank in modern times. It would seem that some chieftains were buried with their chariots or ponies, as was perhaps the case at Newnham Croft, Cambridge, where the contracted skeleton of a middle⁄aged man was found with brooches, an imported arm⁄ring and part of the head⁄harness of a pony, equipment that can be dated to the second century B.C. An extended human skeleton of similar date was found long ago at Mildenhall, possibly under a barrow, and he lay with his long iron sword, an axe and a gold torc between the skeletons of his two ponies. Other inhumations can also be attributed to the Marnians. At Shouldham in west Norfolk an extended

Plate 23

skeleton was found with an iron sword having a pommel knob in the form of a gloomy human face; this burial is almost certainly that of a Marnian warrior of the late third century B.C. A child's body with a ribbed bronze bracelet, discovered at Icklingham, may be a native-born descendant of one of these immigrants; farther south-west, the Chronicle Hills barrows at Whittlesford, Cambridgeshire, covered iron-nailed coffins containing double inhumations, a custom paralleled in the Marne area.

Some of the pottery of this phase, such as a bowl from Risby, Suffolk, is comparable with that from the Marne, indicating that some women accompanied their menfolk when they settled in East Anglia. Other Marnians obviously married local girls, who tried to adapt their traditional pottery to suit the tastes of their new lords, thus initiating a hybrid culture. The clothing of these people was probably secured by flattened-bow bronze brooches, several examples of which have been found at Lakenheath and Mildenhall. The retinue of the Marnian chieftains doubtless included armourers, whose skills were essential to the supremacy of their masters in a conquered land. Expert metalworkers from overseas set up workshops where they and their apprentices made swords, daggers, spears, shields, fittings for chariots and the ponies which drew them, and insignia for the embellishment of chieftains and their high priests. The artistic style in which this fine metalwork was ornamented owed its introduction to the tastes of the invaders, but later developed on insular lines. Its outstanding products belong to the third and last phase of the Iron Age from 150 B.C. onwards, but the foundations of these schools of craftsmanship were laid in the late third and early second centuries B.C., when the Marnian aristocracy was carving out its land holdings. In East Anglia, their sway extended from Cambridgeshire through Breckland into Norfolk, but does not seem to have reached the Ipswich region, where the Iron Age A peasantry of Phase I continued their placid existence. Their subjugation was to come later, when they were overcome by the Belgae who formed the final group in the cultural amalgam of Iron Age East Anglia.

The Belgae were a powerful confederation of tribes of Ger' manic origin, though their language was Celtic; they came from eastern France and Belgium, chiefly south of the Ardennes. Alone among the tribes of Gaul they were able to repel the assaults of the Cimbri and Teutones in 110 B.C., but the in' security created by this invasion may have influenced many of them to cross the Channel about ten years later and settle in south'east England, thus introducing our Iron Age C culture. These Belgic tribesmen soon established themselves in Kent and southern Essex and spread into Hertfordshire, where they emerge into history as the Catuvellauni who, in the next century, became the dominant power in Britain. This was a mass movement of warlike farmers and craftsmen, who, sword in one hand, sickle in the other, established farms and *oppida* (tribal capitals defended by banks and ditches). The newcomers introduced wheel'made pottery, especially elegant pedestal urns of great technical and artistic excellence. They often cleared stretches of woodland to create farms on the heavy loams which they cultivated with the aid of broad'bladed ploughshares and coulters capable of turning a sod, unlike the light ploughs of their predecessors which had merely scratched the surface. Although Caesar was inclined to regard the Belgic people he met as the most civilized of the British, the scattered, flimsy huts of a Belgic tribal capital must have seemed the negation of Roman ideas of town planning. Only the presence of industries and the scale of the widespread commerce, necessitating the use of coinage, attest the urban status of these settlements. Before we survey the expansion of this Belgic kingdom into an empire and the spread of its cultural influence into East Anglia, the state of that territory during Phase III—the two centuries pre' ceding the Roman invasion of A.D. 43—must be considered.

We have noted, during Phase II, the arrival of the Marnian warriors who established themselves as a ruling class over the Iron Age A peasantry and minor chiefs of the Cambridge region, Breckland and west Norfolk, while the inhabitants of the Sandlings of south-east Suffolk remained immune from their influence. The cultural distinctions between these two areas, separated by the afforested belt of High Suffolk, are reflected in their political organization, as recorded by Caesar. In 54 B.C. he mentions the Trinovantes whose tribal area probably included the Ipswich and Colchester regions, while the 'Cenimagni', who sent envoys to Caesar with their submission, are probably to be identified with the Iceni, whose sway ex- tended over Norfolk and north-west Suffolk. The beginning of this tribal system is uncertain and may go back to the initial Iron Age A occupation, reflecting the diverse origins of the settlers in the two regions. The independent cultural develop- ment of the Breckland and Ipswich regions has been shown in earlier chapters to be a distinctive feature of East Anglian pre- history—it survives today as two separate county councils for Suffolk. Though the Trinovantes were one of the most power- ful tribes in the south-east of England during the mid-first century B.C., they were obviously being harassed by their Belgic neighbours of Hertfordshire, since Caesar records the arrival of a Trinovantian king as a refugee from the attacks of Cassivellaunus, king of the Catuvellauni. The tribal capital of the Trinovantes was probably at, or close to, Camulodunum on the outskirts of modern Colchester, but it is by no means clear that the Iceni, for their part, possessed similar headquarters. The concentration of population in west Norfolk and north- west Suffolk would suggest that this area was the Iceni's centre of power and the probable seat of its monarchy, but no such site has yet been detected. It must be remembered, how- ever, that the south-western boundary of their territory before the issue of coinage is unknown, and in the early first century B.C.

may have included the hillforts on the Gog Magog Hills near Cambridge, one of which could have been its tribal capital. The existence of another concentration of population, located in the Norwich district, suggests that the kingdom of the Iceni may have been formed from the amalgamation of two separate tribal groups, and it is possible that the headquarters of this eastern group was Tasburgh Camp. From the latter years of the first century B.C. to *c.* A.D. 50, Icenian coins give in an abbreviated form the names of their kings, though their monarchy may have been of considerably greater antiquity, beginning perhaps with some of the Marnian chieftains.

Besides imposing their social organization on the Iron Age A peasantry, the Marnian chiefs of the Iceni and their descen⁄dants were responsible for many spectacular innovations in the material culture of the area. Their martial propensities demanded weapons, chariots and elaborately accoutred ponies; their wealth required social recognition in the form of lavish orna⁄ments, often of precious metals. Their artistic instincts exacted the highest standard of craftsmanship in the production of this equipment, which was decorated in a manner at once aesthetically satisfying and magically effective, and hoards of this type of material have been found at Ringstead, Santon and Snettisham in west Norfolk.

The continued vitality of the tradition of chariot warfare is shown by the recovery from the Icenian tribal area of linch⁄pins for securing chariot⁄wheels. These have been found at Thorn⁄ham and near Marham and in the Santon hoard, which also contained six bronze nave⁄bands. From Burwell in north⁄east Cambridgeshire comes the bronze cap from a charioteer's handgrip, while linch⁄pins from Westhall in north⁄east Suffolk suggest that these vehicles were also in use among the Trinovantes. This Westhall hoard, perhaps from the site of a harness⁄room, has yielded valuable evidence for the gay caparison of the ponies which drew the chariots. It contained eight enamelled terret/rings as well as two bronze harness/mounts brilliantly enamelled in red and blue, perhaps the trappings of a chieftain's pair/in/hand. Similar pony/harness fittings, also dating from the very end of the Iron Age and showing Belgic influence, have been recovered from at least five sites in Breckland; these suggest that the use of chariots was widespread among the local nobility. A fine pair of bridle/bits in bronze and iron,

Plate 24

with three links in the Yorkshire manner, came from the Ringstead hoard and date from *c.* 50 B.C. Other bronze bits with two links, a type found in south/west England and dating from the early first century A.D., come from Elveden and Santon.

A few weapons have survived from this last phase of the Iron Age in East Anglia. A long iron sword dredged from the River Wissey at Stoke Ferry, Norfolk, may be as old as the late second century B.C., while another from Lakenheath, still in its elegant bronze sheath, probably dates from the following century. A decorated loop from a sword scabbard of the early first century A.D., coming from Icklingham, completes the list of offensive armament recorded from this area. Two semicircular bronze plates, ornamented with studs of shell or tufa and probably from an oblong shield, were found in the Ringstead hoard.

East Anglia is relatively poor in military accoutrements, but extraordinarily rich in objects of personal adornment. From the series of hoards unearthed by ploughing at Ken Hill, Snettisham, in 1948–50, has come the largest accumulation of precious metal so far recorded from Iron Age Britain. Prior to concealment by a metalsmith who had begun to convert some of it into new ornaments, the most spectacular part of this

Plate 25

treasure—the gold torcs—must, from the magnificence of the style and the intrinsic value of the metal, have been the property of a priestly corporation or the regalia of a royal dynasty, either of the Iceni or their neighbours. Some of the material in this find came from the area between south Suffolk and the Thames and little of the remainder need have been made at or near Snettisham. The discovery at Bawsey and North Creake, also in north-west Norfolk, of torcs of gold alloyed with silver and copper indicates that personal insignia of this type were used in the area in the latter part of the first century B.C. This strengthens the case for regarding these Snettisham finds as testimony to the power and wealth of the local dynasty. This group of hoards contained over fifty torcs (bracelets or necklets), more than from all the rest of Britain, together with rings of gold alloy, bronze or tin, worn on the thumb or toe. Other metal objects for personal use surviving from East Anglia include two disc brooches dating from the middle of the first century A.D. found in the Santon and Westhall hoards, the former bearing a winged griffin and the latter a pony.

Fig. 27 Disc brooch. Santon, Norfolk. Scale 4/3

The Belgic invasion of *c.* 100 B.C. introduced coinage to south-eastern England, and barter gradually gave way to a monetary economy, but its diffusion outside the Belgic-occupied areas was slow. The earliest coins known from East Anglia, dating from soon after 100 B.C., were the crude cast discs of tin and copper alloy—known as 'speculum'—found in the Snettisham Treasure. These were products of a non-Belgic group in the south-east of England and were only scrap metal when brought to East Anglia nearly a century later. A few gold coins of the tribe of the Bellovaci were imported from northern France at the same date as the speculum coins were cast. Some of these have been found as scrap at Snettisham, while others in the Ipswich region suggest trade and perhaps Belgic settlement. A hoard of gold coins of the Gaulish tribe of the Atrebates, found at Haverhill, Suffolk, was probably imported between 100 and 75 B.C., and this type formed the model for many British-minted coins. Other imports of similar date include a hoard of gold coins from Belgium revealed by coastal erosion at Weybourne in north Norfolk. Before 50 B.C. a few locally minted gold staters with a design derived from the

Fig. 28 Disc brooch. Westhall, Suffolk. Scale 4/3

head of the god Apollo on one side and a disjointed horse on the other began to circulate in northern East Anglia. A variety confined to Norfolk transforms the horse into a wolf or boar. During the latter part of the first century B.C., the Iceni were minting a plentiful supply of gold and silver coins with an Apollo pattern; they have an uncouth human head or a boar on the obverse and a prancing horse on the reverse. A series of inscribed silver coins were produced from about the birth of Christ until after the Roman invasion, and those bore the shortened names of six kings of the tribe. Many of these Icenian coins have been recovered from hoards found at Freckenham and Santon Downham, Suffolk, and from Honingham and Weston in Norfolk. Gold coins bearing the name of king Addedomarus of the Trinovantes, who reigned from *c*. 15 B.C. to the end of the century, have been found in the tribal area of south-east Suffolk and adjacent parts of Essex.

The representation of the boar on some Icenian coins may indicate that it was an object of veneration, but it would be as unwise to speculate on this as on the meaning of Boudicca's appeal to the goddess 'Andraste' in A.D. 60–61. There is no direct evidence for Druids in East Anglia at this date, but the amount of pottery of the early first century A.D. from the Arminghall henge-monument suggests a revival of religious practice at this ancient sanctuary.

It is now time to recount the impact on the Iceni and the Trinovantes of Belgic expansion between the invasions of Caesar (55–54 B.C.) and Claudius (A.D. 43). In Caesar's day the Catuvellauni had been harassing the Trinovantes in north-east Essex but were ordered to desist as part of the settlement imposed by the Romans. A generation later the Catuvellauni disregarded this when their king, Tasciovanus, seized Camulo-dunum soon after his accession (*c*. 20–15 B.C.); but he was speedily driven out by the Trinovantian king, Addedomarus.

Checked in this direction, Tasciovanus thrust northwards from his headquarters at Verulamium (St Albans) into Cambridgeshire and Northamptonshire. The issue of an Icenian coin inscribed CAMUL may be evidence for a temporary seizure of Camulodunum by the Iceni; if so, it was but a tran/sient success, for by A.D. 1 that much/fought/over *oppidum* was seized by another Belgic monarch, Dubnovellaunus of Kent, and Trinovantian independence came to an end. During the next few years Belgic farmers spread over the Trinovantian area of south/east Suffolk, at least as far north as Burgh/by/Wood/bridge. They occupied the sparsely populated Stour valley, as is shown by the discovery there of their characteristic wheel/made pottery and cremation cemeteries such as the one at Boxford. The fortress at Clare may have been erected in an attempt to halt this colonization.

Plate 26

However, the tribulations of Camulodunum were not yet at an end. By A.D. 10 Dubnovellaunus in his turn had been driven out by Cunobelinus, who, succeeding his father Tasciovanus, transferred his capital to the city he had conquered, making it the corner/stone of the most powerful kingdom in Britain. Clearly it would soon be the turn of the culturally backward Iceni to be absorbed into this Belgic empire. Before this fate became imminent the lower culture began to be influenced by the higher, as can be seen in the modification of some Icenian pottery, imitating cordons on Belgic wheel/turned wares, in the adoption of enamelling on pony harness and in the addition of the monarch's name to the tribal coinage. But these cultural contacts and the activities of individual craftsmen must not be allowed to obscure the essential hostility between the Belgic empire and the Iceni, whose own frontier zone in Cambridgeshire had already been seized. Warned by these acts of aggression, some Icenian chieftains made prepara/tions to resist any further advance, and it is possible that the following fortresses owe their present form to this threat: the

Plate 27

outworks of Thetford Castle (later incorporated into the defences of the Norman motte and bailey castle), Warham Camp, Holkham Camp and Wighton. But only the first of these is likely ever to have seen the invaders, for the Belgic-Icenian frontier on the eve of the Roman invasion was probably the Little Ouse river. A recent discovery at Snailwell, near Newmarket, has considerably strengthened the evidence for Belgic overlords in Breckland just before the Roman conquest of A.D. 43. This find comprised a grave containing a couch or litter ornamented with bronze plating, on which the cremated bones of a dead chieftain with his bronze armlet had been placed. At the side of the couch had been laid a shield, a bronze bowl, three amphorae (wine-jars), and a group of pottery ewers, cups, bowls, beakers and flagons. At its foot were joints of pig, ox and fowl, which, together with the pottery, suggest the remains of a funeral feast. Almost all the pottery and many other objects in this rich grave group had been imported from Gaul, doubtless through Camulodunum, during the time of Cunobelinus's supremacy there (*c.* A.D. 10–40/43). Another cremation burial of about the same date, found with pottery and a bronze-mounted tankard at Elveden, near Thetford, lends further weight to the suggestion that this area was controlled by Belgic chieftains, rather than by Icenian aristocrats.

Thus, on the eve of the Claudian invasion of A.D. 43, that section of the Trinovantes which dwelt in the Ipswich region was subject to the Catuvellauni, and their basic Iron Age A culture had become belgicized by the influence of these new and progressive farmers. The Suffolk portion of Breckland had only recently been overrun by Belgic tribesmen, and the Iceni to the north were doubtless apprehensive of farther expansion beyond the Little Ouse along the line of the Icknield Way. The Icenian tribal headquarters had perhaps been moved northwards to the coast, where warriors were digging in, prepared for a fight to the death against the seemingly irresistible power of the Catuvellauni. It did not seem that the end could be long deferred, but when news of the Roman landing in Kent reached them, with the implication that their powerful enemy was now compelled to fight for his life, fresh hope must have dawned at the Icenian royal court. This hope of continued independence was to prove a short-lived illusion.

CHAPTER VII

The Roman Age

THE STORY OF ROMAN EAST ANGLIA is based largely
on archaeological discoveries, supplemented somewhat
fitfully by historical records. The latter tell us that for most of
the Roman period (A.D. 43–425) the whole of East Anglia
formed part of one province of a vast empire, stretching from
the Irish Sea to the Euphrates, and from the forests of Germany
to the deserts of North Africa. The sheer bulk of the surviving
archaeological material, more extensive than from all previous
ages together, indicates a significant increase of population. At
the beginning of the period the people were still firmly rooted
in their old prehistoric centres, but they soon spread into the
Fens and on to the rich clay soils, where they cleared considerable areas of forest. This demonstration of Man's increasing
dominance over nature is also apparent in the construction for
the first time of metalled highways, forming an efficient system
of communications, and in the effective drainage of the Fens
by the digging of canals. In pre-Roman times the economy was
predominantly rural; now, towns with merchants, shopkeepers
and artisans, and ports with facilities for merchantmen and
warships were imposed upon this rural economy. Hovels of
timber and thatch were supplemented by elegant buildings in
masonry, the materials for which were sometimes transported
hundreds of miles. Many household crafts were superseded by
specialized industrial production, and even remote East Anglian
farmsteads were flooded with the factory-made crockery of
France. Yet spectacular as these innovations were in the every-
day life of the population of Roman East Anglia, they did not
involve a mass immigration of foreigners into the area. We
should not therefore rush to the opposite extreme and regard the
Roman Age as merely a continuation of the Iron Age under

new management. It was instead a fusion of the two cultures implicit in the term 'Romano-British'. The language of the rural peasantry doubtless remained Celtic until the arrival of Teutonic-speaking migrants who, late in the period, settled in parts of East Anglia, but Latin was the official language of administration and commerce, and workmen's graffiti show that its use was widespread in towns.

The Belgic kingdoms, products of the disintegration of the empire of Cunobelinus, took the initial impact of the Roman invasion of A.D. 43, and suffered accordingly. After retreating north of the Thames, the Belgic forces were again defeated by the Roman army under the personal command of the Emperor Claudius, who, within a fortnight, led his triumphant forces into the native capital of Camulodunum to receive the surrender of the Catuvellauni. This submission implies that the whole of the former Trinovantian tribal area, subject to the Catuvellauni for a generation, was at once incorporated in the newly formed province. Just how far effective Roman control extended at this time we have no means of knowing, but it seems likely that south-east Suffolk came within the Roman orbit, the thick woodlands of High Suffolk providing a frontier between the new Roman state and the Iceni. This 'brave and warlike people', perhaps led by their monarch, whose abbreviated name—SAEMU—appears on coins of about this date, sought and were granted a treaty of friendship with Rome, a move which secured the right flank of the Roman army before its advance into the Midlands. The Roman commander estab-lished a fortified frontier—the Fosse Way line—from the Severn to the Trent, to secure this area against raids by tribes as yet unconquered. It was now apparent to the Iceni that the Roman power, which had saved them from absorption by the Catuvellauni, would in its turn engulf them. In alliance with their neighbours, probably the Coritani of the Midlands, they rose in A.D. 47–48 and concentrated their forces in a specially built fortress where they received the attack of the Roman army, and, with the courage of desperation, went down fighting, overcome at the last by the superior military skill of the in, vaders. No further details of this abortive revolt are known, but it may be surmised that Roman troops moved temporarily into northern East Anglia to disarm those who still resisted. This revolt may also have caused 'Saemu' to be replaced by Prasutagus, regarded as a more reliable ally.

The kingdom of the Iceni remained nominally independent for another dozen years under the guidance of the astute and wealthy Prasutagus. Roman commercial penetration into Icenian territory is apparent at this time. The native coinage now began to be replaced by Roman brass and silver, inscribed with the name of Claudius, and later of Nero, though the finding at Needham of a mould for casting native coins points to sturdy local independence in financial matters. Belgic, inspired pottery made in the Colchester district, and red-glazed Samian ware and other fine pottery from Gaul, imported through the port of Colchester, found an expanding market among the Iceni, where the adoption of Roman ideas was stimulated by ready credit to the Icenian nobility. Native metalworkers not only continued to produce fine enamelled pony-harness fittings for the local aristocracy, like the group found at Saham Toney, Norfolk, but also created new and attractive designs, like the dragonesque bronze brooch found at Lakenheath with an inhumation burial. The strength of native tradition at any site was in direct ratio to its distance from Camulodunum, the political capital of the Roman province and the centre of diffusion of Roman material culture. This influence was there, fore felt most strongly in the Trinovantian area of south-east Suffolk at sites like Coddenham, where refuse pits and traces of timber buildings indicate this spread of romanization between A.D. 43 and 60. But the peaceful absorption of Roman material culture was to be shattered by the violent events of A.D. 60–61, recorded for us by Tacitus and Dio Cassius, when, for a brief spell, the inhabitants of East Anglia dominated the scene and nearly destroyed the new province.

It was the death of Prasutagus, probably in A.D. 60, that precipitated the crisis. As a dependent monarch he was unable to bequeath his kingdom, but in an attempt to ensure that his two daughters should share half of his personal estate, he left the other half of his considerable wealth to the Emperor Nero. But the rapacity of Roman army officers and civil servants frustrated his plan. The tribal area was overrun, loans were called in, the tribal aristocracy was stripped of its inherited wealth and reduced to slavery, the residence of Prasutagus was plundered, his daughters were raped and his widow Boudicca flogged. The Iceni had welcomed the Roman invasion of A.D. 43 as a stick for beating the Catuvellauni, but now they felt cheated, smarting from the arrogance and greed of the Romans as they proceeded to annex the kingdom. The fiery personality of Boudicca, that masterful woman, easily converted this wide-spread disillusion and hatred into a full-scale revolt. She was not lacking for allies: the Trinovantes had from the first been treated as conquered serfs, and their best farmland seized for the foundation of the new provincial capital at Camulodunum, settled by ex-army veterans. While the nameless multitude toiled in farm and building gangs, the native aristocracy was impoverished by contributions towards the maintenance of the cult of the living Emperor Claudius, concentrated in a vast temple. The massive substructure of this temple, which to the Britons, as Tacitus reports, 'seemed the citadel of eternal slavery', may still be seen beneath the Norman castle of Colchester. It was on Camulodunum, unfortified and unprepared, that the full fury of the attack of the Iceni and the Trinovantes fell. The capital was held by a mere two hundred men, and all resistance was over in two days. The town was laid waste, the Temple of Claudius sacked, and there followed an inhuman massacre and

Plate 28

mutilation of the captives, the direst cruelty being reserved for those sacrificed in the sacred groves. The main Roman forces were engaged in subduing Anglesey, while the nearest garrison —the Ninth Legion—was stationed at Lincoln. When news of the revolt reached them part of the Ninth marched and, meeting the rebels, was cut to pieces, only the cavalry escaping. The rebels, gathering strength as they advanced, sacked Londinium and Verulamium, and, as a measure of their hatred, massacred all, Romans and native supporters alike. But retribution was inevitable once the disorderly British masses met the highly disciplined legions marching from Anglesey; and Boudicca, though an inspiring war-leader, was no military genius. At some unknown site north-west of London, possibly in Northamptonshire, the opposing forces met. The javelins and short swords of the legionaries, and the lances of the cavalry wrought fearful slaughter among the rebels, whose field of manœuvre was circumscribed by an ill-sited wagon-park. Boudicca escaped to die by sickness or by poison, and the kingdom of the Iceni was at an end. The penalty for rebellion was now due.

Once the Roman army had been reinforced from the con-tinent, East Anglia was invaded and laid waste by fire and the sword. Temporary forts were constructed at Great Chesterford, Pakenham, Coddenham and doubtless at other sites, for the troops engaged in this subjugation. Farms and huts went up in flames, sanctuaries like Arminghall were desecrated, whilst hoards such as those from Santon, Westhall and Honingham were buried for safety. Some of the Iceni may have held out for a time in the hope of securing better terms, for the excessive severity of the governor, Suetonius, led to his recall after a governmental inquiry. Under a milder governor the Iceni settled down to rebuild their shattered economy. During the long months of the insurrection they had neglected their farms, and famine was now added to their other tribulations. It is likely that the harsh measures of Suetonius also included the deportation to Fenland, flooded and uninhabited throughout the Iron Age, of thousands of rebellious Iceni and their allies. There, as convict gangs, they were set to labour on drainage works to create farmland. These punitive measures were so effective that the troops engaged in the pacification probably did not remain in the area for more than a few months, but the revolt had shaken the Roman government so deeply that precautions were taken to ensure that any new rising would be suppressed at once. These included the construction on the coast at Thornham of a signal station, visible from the Lincolnshire Wolds, behind which, at Lincoln, was the fortress of the Ninth Legion. The troops were ready to return to East Anglia should the situation warrant, but fortunately it was never necessary. Henceforth the only soldiers in East Anglia were retired veterans or troops on leave, and two whole centuries free from war gave an impetus to civilized development.

Plate 29

The chief unit for the administration of the countryside was the *civitas*, corresponding roughly to a modern county and based on the old tribal group. Apart from its magistrates, the inhabitants were not Roman citizens like those in a purely Roman settlement, such as the *colonia* for retired soldiers established at Camulodunum in A.D. 49–50. The adminis- trative centre, or cantonal capital, often bore the name of the tribe, as in *Venta Icenorum* (Caistor-by-Norwich), and the survivors of the old tribal aristocracy were in charge of the canton's affairs and property, with powers of levying local taxation and responsible to the central government for the collection of imperial taxes. The boundaries of the district governed from Caistor are uncertain, but it may well have corresponded with the former Icenian tribal area of Norfolk and north-west Suffolk. South-east Suffolk, on the other hand, probably formed part of the canton of the Trinovantes; the boundaries of this canton are, however, as obscure at this time

Fig. 29

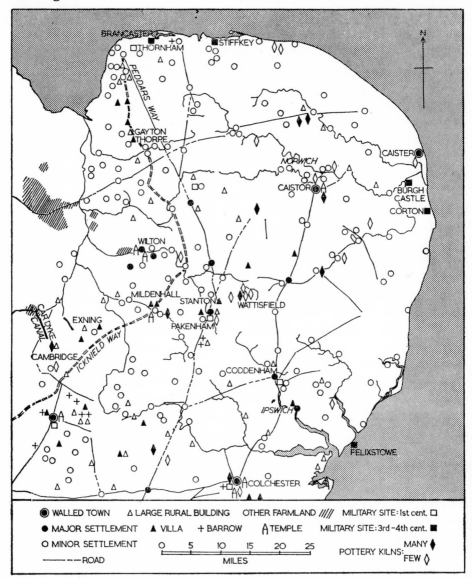

Fig. 29   Distribution of Roman culture

as is the site of the administrative centre for which, among others, Camulodunum and Coddenham have been suggested.

The process of romanization in material culture, begun in the Claudian period and rudely shattered by the Boudiccan revolt, spread during the decade 60–70. However, owing to the harsh repression of the revolt and consequent depopulation, East Anglia lagged behind other parts of southern Britain in both the speed and intensity of this romanization, which only became normal in the early years of the second century. One of the first products of this policy was the construction of metalled roads, by native labour gangs under military engineers, to supplement the existing system of native trackways. Roman roads in East Anglia are ill-explored and imperfectly preserved owing to subsequent robbing of the structure, but it is clear that not all were laid out at the same date nor for the same purpose. Only a few have been dated by excavation; the main road from Camulodunum to Caistor-by-Norwich was built about the year 70, with posting stations for changing horses at, for instance, Stoke Ash and Scole, and with timber bridges for river crossings.

About this time was begun the construction of the small cantonal capital and market town at Caistor-by-Norwich. It occupied a level site of about 50 acres on the east bank of the Tas, though whether it replaced any native settlement of importance in the vicinity is unknown. For the last generation of the first century A.D. it was an unpretentious agglomeration of small huts set amidst a grid-iron pattern of streets, little better than the capital of Cunobelinus had been half a century before. Smaller settlements, like Saham Toney-Threxton, Ixworth and Brettenham, gradually came into existence on main roads during this latter part of the first century, while earlier foundations such as Coddenham, where a statue to Nero perhaps indicates a shrine or temple, were rebuilt.

In the countryside, small circular huts were still being built

Plate 30

Plate 37

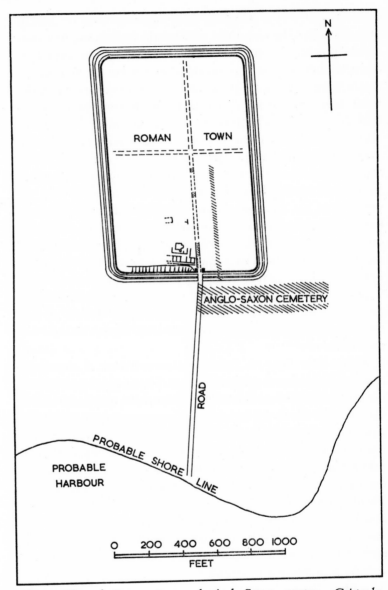

Fig. 30 Plan of Roman town and Anglo-Saxon cemetery. Caister-by-
Yarmouth, Norfolk

on or adjacent to the sites of Iron Age farms, or on freshly cleared land. The technique of farming during the first two centuries of Roman occupation remained that of the latter part of the Iron Age. There is evidence during these last years of the first century for expanding industrial activity in the countryside. Briquetage and clay‚lined tanks at Wolferton and Runcton Holme in west Norfolk show that saline water was being distilled to produce salt for the preservation of foodstuffs. Although much pottery was imported from Colchester and from abroad, coarse wares were produced locally in kilns, such as those at Morley St Peter, Norfolk, by professional potters whose products had now superseded the housewife's domestic handiwork. The production of iron from the local sands and gravels may have begun in the Iron Age, but the earliest definite evidence for the exploitation of these low‚grade ores comes from the late first century A.D. site at Ranworth, Norfolk.

At the turn of the century the pace of romanization began to quicken in both town and country. The first fruits of this new expansive policy are seen at Caister‚by‚Yarmouth, where a new town and port was founded *c*. 125 close to a sheltered harbour. The siting of a port here provided the shortest sea‚ crossing to the mouth of the Rhine, and was doubtless intended for the developing trade with the Rhineland which included such goods as lava millstones and glassware. At first, Caister's defences were a timber palisade backed by a clay rampart, but about the middle of the second century this was replaced by a substantial flint wall 10 feet thick. Late in the century a large building, interpreted as a boarding‚house for seamen, was erected inside the south gate. Masonry was used for public buildings at Caistor‚by‚Norwich even earlier than this. About 125 the *forum* (market‚place) and the *basilica* (town‚hall) were erected on a central site about 200 feet wide, with a colonnaded façade overlooking a gravelled street. Two blocks farther west the public baths, supplied by a wooden pipe‚line, were also

Fig. 30

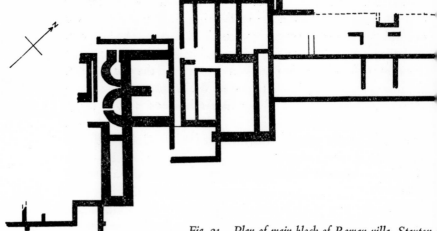

Fig. 31   Plan of main block of Roman villa. Stanton,

built at about this time. To the north of these municipal buildings industrial activity was permitted, and at least four pottery kilns were functioning from about 110 to 140. The population may now have increased to about 1,000 and new houses were being erected in a romanized manner on a rec-tangular plan with a modest bath, though in nothing more substantial than wattle-and-daub. As in most Roman towns in Britain there was no sewerage system, except for soak-away urinals made from disused wine-jars. At the very end of the century, perhaps as part of a general move to put the province in a state of defence, a massive wall, 11 feet thick and some 20 feet high, of concrete faced with squared flint and brick, was constructed round the central area of the town, enclosing some 35 acres and truncating some of the earlier streets. This curtain wall was backed by an earthen bank and reinforced externally, possibly later, by rectangular and U-shaped towers and by a ditch, 80 to 100 feet wide, crossed by timber bridges at the gateways.

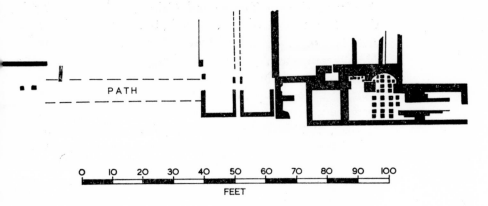

The story of the countryside in the second century is still imperfectly known, but an impetus towards the adoption of a romanized style of building can be discerned here, as in the towns, from about the reign of Hadrian (117–138). There seems little evidence for building in masonry until the latter half of the century; earlier, the new farmhouses were probably rectangular timber-framed structures like one recently excavated at Exning, Suffolk, which was reconstructed with a flint and mortar wall base only in the late second or early third century. After *c.* 150, many farmhouses were constructed which varied in size, plan and architectural embellishment according to the status and wealth of the occupants. The dwellings included simple cottages for labourers, not much larger than a single modern room, larger, barn-like structures inhabited both by working farmers and their stock, and large houses to which the term 'villa' is best applied. These residences of the country gentry were built with masonry footings, mosaic floors, bath-houses and heated rooms, and were adorned with painted plaster walls and glazed windows; there were auxiliary buildings for the farming activities on which the wealth of the estate depended. Most of the East Anglian villa estates, such as West Newton,

Appleton, Gayton Thorpe and Grimston, lie in the fertile Good Sand region of west Norfolk, but others, like Lopham and Tivetshall, are scattered over the heavier soils of south Norfolk; only a few, like that at Whitton (Ipswich), occur in the former Trinovantian area. East Anglia was an area of comfor, table, but not opulent, farmers who were actively engaged in wresting a living from the soil. The size of the buildings at Stanton, Suffolk (at least 300 feet long), suggests an unusually large estate, and here the austere living quarters may indicate the residence of a bailiff, managing the estate for an absentee landlord, possibly the government. These country estates were probably worked by slave-labour which was accommodated in detached quarters. Nothing is known of the field systems associated with any of the Roman farms on the uplands of East Anglia, though it is probable that they were similar to the small native fields of which traces have survived in the Fens. Chance survivals of cereals from Caistor-by-Norwich show that spelt, bread wheat and oats were grown near that town, while barley has been found in a hut at Wangford in north-west Suffolk. Remains of bread wheat found at Littleport, Cambridgeshire, show that conditions in the Fens were now suitable for the cultivation of cereals.

The scale of Roman agricultural activity in Fenland was one of the major archaeological discoveries of the last generation. It has been suggested above that the decision to colonize this waste was taken by the Roman government as part of the suppression of Boudicca's revolt. Excavation of the Car Dyke, near Cottenham, Cambridgeshire, has shown that this canal, for both drainage and navigation, was constructed soon after the middle of the first century, and was intended for barges carrying foodstuffs, probably corn, northwards for the garrisons at Lincoln and, later, York. This canal was, like other canals and main roads in Fenland, clearly the product of military engineering. The wattle-and-daub farmsteads, the droveways

Fig. 31

and the fields, to be seen so clearly from the air, are plainly of native inspiration, even though the whole area may have been an imperial domain subject to central planning. Two types of fields have been identified—the normal rectangular Celtic field and the long strip similar to the Medieval type—and this may show that some Belgae, accustomed to the long strip as the field unit, were sent here with the Iceni to expiate the crime of rebellion. This Fenland agriculture is mainly concentrated on the siltlands south of the Wash in Lincolnshire, but there are few areas of the silt fens without some indication of such activity, especially along the levees of old waterways. In Norfolk, the main areas lie south and west of Downham Market and seem to have been developed in the early second century, whilst extensive occupation by peasant cultivators is also apparent on the banks of The Wellstream at Welney, and at Hockwold-cum-Wilton in the Little Ouse valley.

Plate 31

The twin demands of agricultural expansion and building in town and country in the second century called for a corre-sponding industrial development. Expanding population led to an increasing demand for cheap crockery, and numerous kilns were established, mainly in the boulder-clay country where the necessary fuel (charcoal) was available. Over twenty kilns have been found in and near Wattisfield in north Suffolk, nine at West Stow in the Lark valley and five at Hevingham, north of Norwich. The local iron was now worked more systemati-cally, especially in the Greensand Belt of west Norfolk where traces of smelting are common; five shaft furnaces of this date have recently been investigated at Ashwicken. Quarrying must have taken place on a considerable scale, not only for the raw material for iron smelting, but also for the flint, hard chalk and sandstone used in large quantities for building. The transport of this bulky material must have involved an extensive fleet of barges and probably coasters as well.

The rising standard of living required a wide range of

imports to supplement the products of local industry, and these came from other parts of Britain and abroad. From Dorset came Kimeridge shale table-furnishings and spindle whorls; from the Somerset area blue lias, and from Sussex calcite mud-stone, both for mosaic floors; from the East Midlands and south Yorkshire quernstones; and from many localities distinctive pottery. From Gaul came shiploads of red-glazed Samian ware and bronze *paterae* for heating wine and food; from the quarries of Italy and the Pyrenees white and green marbles for building; from the glasshouses of the East Mediterranean jugs and bowls; and from the mints of Rome and Lyons the great volume of coinage needed for the effective working of this international economy.

Preoccupied by the activities of the living, we have as yet given no attention to the dead. By the late first century cremation was again the universal rite, continuing in vogue until the third century, when it gave place to inhumation. No Roman cremation cemeteries have been fully excavated in East Anglia, but the few known to us suggest that the jars containing the cremated bones were laid out in rows. Isolated cremations also occur. The remains are sometimes associated with a coin—the fee to the ferryman at the River Styx—a bead or, rarely, a mirror. In stoneless areas most memorials to the dead have long perished, though one type remains; this is the barrow, the main British concentration of which lies on the borders of the East Midlands and East Anglia. Nine of these enormous mounds formerly existed at Ashdon in north-west Essex, where the tallest of what are now the Bartlow Hills was over 40 feet high. Some of the four barrows standing in a line at Rougham, Suffolk, contained tiled cists with pottery, glass, iron lamps and a wooden casket, whilst another had a chamber of flint and tile enclosing a lead coffin with a body wrapped in skins. These may be the family vaults of the wealthy occupants of the building found near by. A mound, at Burnham Thorpe, Norfolk, excavated in 1862, is another barrow of Roman date. These conspicuous burial-places all date from the second century or early third century, and the custom of barrow burial is more likely to be an introduction from eastern Belgium, where another large group exists, than a survival from the British Iron Age. Whether those interred are native aristocrats or Belgian immi/ grants is uncertain.

During the third century there was considerable building in the East Anglian towns. At Caistor-by-Norwich, *c.* 200–220, two Romano-Celtic temples were erected side by side with central towers perhaps 50 feet high and surrounding porticos. The wattle-and-daub houses, probably incorporating shops, were now replaced by more substantial buildings with masonry footings and bases for roof-timbers, while the public baths were reconstructed. At the end of the century, the erection of a glass annealing-oven introduced a new industry to the town. Despite this burst of constructional activity, the inhabitants were content to leave the *forum* in ruins from *c.* 200 to 270, when it was re/ built on a smaller scale. Similar neglect is apparent at the south gate, where the guardrooms went out of use and served as refuse tips. A Romano-Celtic temple and other buildings, surrounded by a precinct wall with an imposing entrance, were erected outside the town walls, probably during this century. In the absence of inscriptions, little is known of the deities who inhabited these sanctuaries, but they were probably old native gods assimilated with their Roman counterparts from Gaul and the Rhineland. A hint of the oriental cults that became popular in the third century is provided by a bust of Helioserapis from a priest's cache buried *c.* 260 at Felmingham in north Norfolk, probably close to a rural shrine.

In the countryside, the bigger estates continued to prosper, and were probably expanded by the purchase of some of the adjacent small-holdings, for it is noticeable that a number of small farms, like those at Needham and at Scole in south

Norfolk, were no longer inhabited after the early years of the third century. It may be that these peasants were dispossessed when their arable land was converted to sheep walk, for the presence of carding combs for wool at several sites in Breckland and at Caistor-by-Norwich suggests a thriving woollen industry. But the peasants had problems other than purely economic ones; higher rainfall and lower temperatures in the late Roman period made harvesting difficult, and led to the installation of crop-drying furnaces at fenside settlements like Runcton Holme and Setchey. Suitable fuel was lacking in Fenland for crop-drying and brine evaporation and necessitated the import of coal from Durham, Yorkshire or the East Midlands to farmsteads at Welney. Here a disaster occurred *c*. 275, perhaps due to a tidal surge or the breaching of coastal defences, if such existed. Six feet of silt, deposited over the inhabited areas, have been found elsewhere to contain human skeletons, probably the remains of victims of this severe flood.

Inhumation was the normal burial rite by the end of the third century, but late Roman cemeteries are not easy to identify unless the bodies are accompanied by pottery or adorned with bracelets or other personal decorations. The more wealthy members of the community were occasionally interred in a coffin of lead, or as at Icklingham, of Barnack ragstone.

During the last generation of the third century, the Channel became infested with Saxon pirates who harassed both its shores. To combat this threat, the Roman government ordered the construction of heavily defended fortresses close to harbours suitable as bases for naval squadrons. On the British side this chain of fortified naval bases stretches from the Wash to the Solent, and three of them are known in East Anglia. Brancaster (Branodunum) guarded the approaches to the Wash and the fertile granary that lay behind it; Burgh Castle (Gariannonum) overlooked the commercial harbour of Caister-by-Yarmouth, and lay astride the river route to the cantonal capital; Felixstowe

(Walton Castle) secured the estuaries of the Deben, Stour, Orwell and Colne. All of these sites have yielded some indica-tions of occupation before the last years of the third century, and earlier harbours may well have been converted for naval use. Architectural variations between these forts suggest the work of various military engineers spread over several years. Brancaster is square with rounded corners, walls 11 feet thick backed by a rampart, and with a wide ditch. Burgh Castle is a quadrilateral of about the same size (6 acres), with walls 9 feet thick and a rampart, but its original plan with rounded angles was modified during construction, and bastions for the mounting of heavy artillery (spring guns) were added. Walton Castle has perished beneath the sea, but drawings of its ruins show that it was rectangular with bastions at the corners. These fortresses were thus capable of repelling a direct assault, but an attack would have indicated the failure of their primary function of despatching warships to destroy raiders before they landed, and of sending out their cavalry garrisons to round up any barbarians who had eluded the naval patrols. The Brancaster garrison may have owned the two remarkable helmets of 'gilding metal' dredged from the River Wensum at Worthing, close to a Roman timber bridge carrying the main east-west road across Norfolk. Both are decorated with classical motifs—sea-dragons, eagle's head and snakes on one, and Mars, Victory and Medusa on the visor-mask of the other. The treatment is, however, barbaric, possibly of local origin but more probably from a workshop on the fringe of the Empire on the Rhine or the Danube. These helmets, probably of third-century date, are not normal military equipment, and it has been suggested that they were used for religious ceremonies or sporting activities.

Plates 32, 33

Plates 34, 35, 40

Shielded by the fleet and the coastal fortresses, East Anglia remained prosperous for the first half of the fourth century. The population of the tribal capital may have been increased by the arrival of a few country landlords, for the villas at Gayton

Thorpe and Appleton, for example, do not appear to have been occupied after *c.* 320 to 330. At Caister-by-Yarmouth, the seamen's boarding-house was restored in the early part of the century; one room was burnt out *c.* 340, but the rest of the building continued in use till the end of the century. At Caistor-by-Norwich the extensive excavations show that occupation after *c.* 360 was on a much diminished scale, and economic decline is apparent. This was accelerated by increasing taxation and by the reluctance of the aristocracy to accept official duties. But despite the abandonment of a few farmhouses early in the century, the rural economy continued to flourish. Because of this, it was easy to make good damage which had resulted from a co-ordinated attack in 367 by the Saxons, together with Picts from Scotland and Scots from Ireland, when the commander of the coastal defences, the Count of the Saxon Shore, was killed. Large villas like those at Stanton and Whitton (Ipswich) were still occupied as late as 395, if only by tenants and slaves, while the wealth of some of the country gentry is well demonstrated by the magnificence

Plate 36

of family silver plate, mainly of early fourth-century Mediterranean origin, such as the Mildenhall Treasure. The less wealthy contented themselves with table services of pewter, and the large number of these found in Breckland and in Fenland indicates the affluence of well-to-do farmers in these areas. Many of the Fenland farms were still occupied *c.* 400, but the periodic floods of brackish water brought to an end, shortly after this date, the exploitation of this fertile tract.

The evidence for religious belief in East Anglia during the fourth century is slight, but the bulk of the population was still pagan and doubtless flocked to rural shrines where the priests celebrated the rites wearing elaborate bronze and silver head-

Plates 41, 42

dresses of the types found at Cavenham in Breckland and Wilton on the edge of the Fens. Though the evidence is scanty, a small proportion of the rural population appears to have been

Christian. This is borne out by inscriptions on spoons from the Mildenhall Treasure, on a lead tank found close to a villa at Icklingham, on a pewter dish from a Fenland farmstead at Welney and on a gold ring from Brancaster. A jet plaque carved with a beckoning figure in a Phrygian cap suggests that the Mithras cult attracted the owner of the villa at Whitton.

Plate 39

Plate 38

Following the military disaster of 367 already mentioned, order was soon restored under Count Theodosius, who brought in fresh troops and reconditioned the defences of the province. In East Anglia, this involved the tightening of the coastguard by the construction of fortlets between the Saxon Shore fortresses, to signal the arrival of raiders and alert the defence. A signal station of this type existed at Corton, near Lowestoft; another probable one was located on a hilltop at Stiffkey and others have either been destroyed by coastal erosion or remain to be identified. We know little of the garrisons which held these forts beyond the fact that in *c.* 400 Brancaster was occupied by Dalmatian cavalry and Burgh Castle by Stablesian cavalry, lately arrived from Holland. But there are hints of the presence of barbarian mercenaries, or *foederati*. The find at Croxton, in south-west Norfolk, of a metal plate of Anglo-Saxon type, probably from the sporran of a kilt and dating from *c.* 375, may indicate the presence of only one raider. However, at many East Anglian sites the discovery in fourth-century deposits of wheel-made Roman pottery decorated according to Saxon taste strongly suggests the presence of Saxons and other barbarians from outside the limits of the Empire. These would have been brought in as *foederati*, with grants of land in exchange for military service. Pottery of this type has come from the fortresses of Burgh Castle and Walton Castle, from the tribal capital at Caistor-by-Norwich and from Breckland and west Norfolk. There is some historical evidence to back this supposition. About 370, Alamanni from the Middle Rhine were transported to some part of Britain for this purpose, while a century before that, Vandals and Burgundians had been settled in Britain, though not, of course, necessarily in East Anglia. On the other hand, this Romano-Saxon pottery may indicate the presence of individual Saxon immigrants, a development of trading from the quays of Caister-by-Yarmouth with tribes across the North Sea. Whichever interpretation is correct, there can be little doubt about the Germanic character of *foederati* brought in *c.* 390 to 400 from Schleswig-Holstein and north-west Germany. This dating of the foundation of our earliest Anglo-Saxon cemeteries is based on the work of continental archaeologists, which places the beginning of these Anglo-Saxon communities half a century earlier than the traditional date of 449. This conception of an 'invasion' of barbarians as mercenaries, brought in at the behest of the Roman government at the end of the fourth century to strengthen the east coast defence against the Picts and Saxons, finds strong support in the location of their settlements. Several are sited by Roman lines of communications; others, like those at Markshall and Caistor-by-Norwich, guard the gates of the adjacent Roman town. It is inconceivable that these Anglo-Saxons were allowed to settle there without the approval of the cantonal government. The mercenaries may sometimes have got out of hand, as is suggested by the discovery of the remains of at least thirty-six people inside a large house, burnt down at Caistor-by-Norwich about 400. Even if organized town life at Caistor ended at the hands of mutinous *foederati*, it was not necessarily so in the rest of romanized East Anglia. It is likely that the coastal fortresses were garrisoned till *c.* 407-8, when a large force was taken to the continent. The isolated province was now bidden to defend itself, but apparently *c.* 417 it became possible to send over from Gaul a field army, which ensured the safety of the remaining walled towns in the south-east until *c.* 425. Though Richborough, one of the coastal fortresses in Kent, seems to have been the headquarters of this ultimate Roman scheme of defence, there is at present no evidence for the re-occupation of the Saxon Shore fortresses on the East Anglian coast, and resistance to barbarian aggression there must have been in the hands of the *foederati*, who formed a sort of local militia. The insecurity of the times is reflected in the many hoards of Roman coins concealed, and we must imagine an increasingly barbarized society, rural rather than urban in character, replacing Roman traditions of government and economy. By 425 the grass was growing over the ruins of towns, forts and country mansions; Fenland farms, once the granary of Roman Britain, were abandoned because of flooding; elsewhere the peasantry were scratching a living from the soil, side by side with barbarians who were constantly reinforced by compatriots from across the North Sea. This obvious collapse of the high culture of Roman Britain and return to conditions as primitive as any since Neolithic days, heralded the period long known as 'The Dark Ages'.

CHAPTER VIII

The Early Saxon Age

THE FOUR CENTURIES following the collapse of Roman government and economy in the early fifth century are among the most fascinating in the story of East Anglia. Much documentary evidence was destroyed in the Late Saxon Age, and the surviving material consists of tantalizingly brief entries in the Anglo-Saxon Chronicle, Bede's summary of the conversion of this area to Christianity, and lists of East Anglian kings and ecclesiastical dignitaries. Much has been learnt about the stages of Anglo-Saxon settlement from the scientific study of the evolution of place-names, but this information is sometimes difficult to equate with either historical or archaeological evidence. The latter is very one-sided, telling us little about the living and much about the dead; the systematic study of this material is still in its infancy, though just beginning to yield suggestive interpretations. Based on this information, the period from 425 to 850 may be conveniently divided into three phases, by the intermediate dates 500 and 650.

At the close of the last chapter we have seen that the first Anglo-Saxon settlements were the result of treaty agreements between the Roman government and barbarian mercenaries before the end of the fourth century. The pottery and other equipment from the cemeteries show that these settlers were principally Angles from Schleswig-Holstein, together with some Saxons from the area between the Elbe and the Weser in north-western Germany, and we have suggested that a massacre at Caistor-by-Norwich, of which traces have been found, was the handiwork of mutinous *foederati*. During the next generation, the Anglo-Saxons became well established at the sites which had been selected for them, tilling the adjacent farmland side by side with the sub-Roman peasantry who still enjoyed reasonable prosperity on their small-holdings. After the last effective link with the Empire had been broken *c.* 425, it is likely that local tyrants, either British or Anglo-Saxon, seized control and attempted to defend the region against the continuing attacks of Picts and Saxons. One of the major raids was defeated in 428-9 by the fighting bishop St Germanus, when he paid a visit from Gaul to Verulamium to deal with a British religious heresy; but the threat remained. It is about this time that the much maligned Vortigern, the provincial governor or 'proud tyrant' according to taste, arranged a further settlement in eastern Britain of Anglo-Saxon *foederati* to counter this threat from the Picts and Saxons. The subsequent revolt of the mercenaries against their paymaster is well known. This violent seizure of power was followed by the arrival of numerous re-inforcements from their continental homelands. These new-comers travelled in great open clinker-built rowing vessels, like the boat 77 feet long found at Nydam in Schleswig-Holstein, or the one found in 1830 at Ashby in north-east Suffolk, which was 54 feet long. All the groups involved in this migration of *c.* 425 to 500 have not yet been differentiated archaeologically, but the pottery evidence indicates considerable diversity. We may visualize boat-loads of warriors and their families crossing during this period from Schleswig-Holstein, north-west Ger-many, the North Frisian Islands and possibly Denmark. The place-name, Swaffham, in west Norfolk and in Cambridge-shire, suggests also the presence of a few Swabians. The details of this mid-fifth-century Anglo-Saxon settlement still elude us, but it is clear that by 500 substantial occupation had taken place in the Norwich area, north and west Norfolk and Breckland. Many of the newcomers had used the rivers leading inland from the Wash to establish themselves round the margins of the Fens, though not in them, for this marshy plain had again become the water-logged wilderness from which Roman technical skill and Icenian labour had created fertile farmland.

Fig. 32

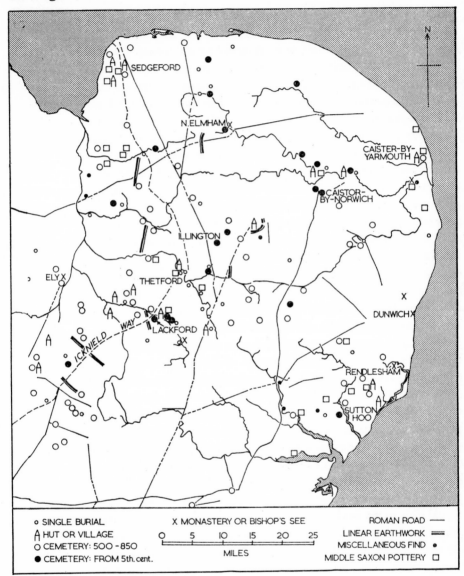

SEDGEFORD

N.ELMHAM

CAISTER-BY-YARMOUTH

CAISTOR-BY-NORWICH

ILLINGTON

ELY

THETFORD

DUNWICH

ICKNIELD WAY

LACKFORD

RENDLESHAM

SUTTON HOO

○ SINGLE BURIAL	X MONASTERY OR BISHOP'S SEE	ROMAN ROAD —
Ⱥ HUT OR VILLAGE		LINEAR EARTHWORK ═
○ CEMETERY: 500 -850		MISCELLANEOUS FIND ●
● CEMETERY: FROM 5th.cent.		MIDDLE SAXON POTTERY □

5 10 15 20 25

MILES

Fig. 32   Distribution of Early Saxon cultures

In the Ipswich region, on the other hand, there are few traces of settlement until the early sixth century; but whether this is due to a mere handful of early Anglo-Saxons having settled here, or to inadequate exploration, is not yet clear. By the mid fifth century it is difficult to identify the descendants of the romanized peasantry who had prospered in East Anglia a few decades earlier. But coins and pottery hint at the continued presence of romanized elements in the population until late in the century. Numismatists have suggested that tiny barbarous copies of Roman bronze coins of the third and fourth centuries were still being struck, and that the hoards of these found at Icklingham in north-west Suffolk, Redenhall in south Norfolk and Tuddenham St Martin near Ipswich, were concealed as late as 450–70. Kilns for the production of Roman wheel-made pottery ceased to function in the early years of the fifth century, but hand-made imitations have been recognized in the cemeteries at Caistor-by-Norwich and Lackford. There are fewer surviving Celtic place-names in East Anglia than in almost any part of southern England, which supports the idea that most of the population may have been speaking a Germanic dialect after the early years of the fifth century. It is unfortunate that cremation was apparently the universal burial rite in the area at this time, so that we cannot distinguish physically between the remains of native and intruder. We may conclude, then, that some of the sub-Roman peasantry perished at the hands of the invaders and others fled westwards, while the bulk stayed as serfs, working the land for Anglo-Saxon farmers and rapidly acquiring their material culture.

The sub-Roman population of the early fifth century may possibly be responsible for the construction of some of the imposing linear earthworks which lie athwart important lines of communication. These barriers, composed of bank and ditch, sometimes run across country for several miles, their ends resting on what were natural obstacles. In Norfolk, the

Bicham Ditch and the Launditch barred traffic along the east-west Roman road, the Fossditch controlled the Drove Road, Bunn's Bank straddles routes to the south of Attle-borough, and the Devil's Ditch traverses Garboldisham Heath; in Suffolk there are only the relatively insignificant Black Ditches on Cavenham Heath. The most impressive of these earthworks in the area is the Devil's Dyke, which lies in Cambridgeshire along the boundary of Newmarket Heath. This formidable obstacle to traffic along the Icknield Way is 7½ miles long, with one end resting on marsh and the other on formerly wooded country, and in its best preserved section measures over 60 feet from the top of the bank to the bottom of the ditch. Despite numerous excavations, especially on the Cambridgeshire examples, these linear earthworks are not accurately dated and may not all be of the same period. There is, however, enough evidence to show that the Devil's Dyke was built after the third century, and that the Fossditch was thrown up after *c*. 390, while none is likely to be later than the early seventh century. These earthworks may have been erected against the encroachments of the Anglo-Saxon *foederati*, or as politico-military barriers connected with the expansion of the East Anglian kingdom (which will be discussed later), or as obstacles to cattle rustling.

It is difficult to estimate the density of population in East Anglia in the fifth century as no cemetery has yet been com-pletely excavated; at the best explored site, Caistor-by-Norwich, there were between 700 and 1,000 burials over a period of about two and a half centuries, suggesting about three deaths a year. Unfortunately, we know almost nothing about either villages or farms built by the Anglo-Saxons in the fifth century. The discovery in north-west Germany of the remains of large timber-framed buildings of this period, similar to the barn-like farm-houses still surviving in that area in which the farmer, his family and his cattle live beneath the same roof, would suggest that similar structures should be found in East Anglia. Small hamlets of one-roomed huts existed in sixth-century East Anglia and similar dwellings were probably being erected for the peasantry even earlier. Impressions of barley on pottery of the fifth and sixth centuries found in the Cambridge region suggests that this crop was important in East Anglia, while oats, flax and woad were probably also grown. Economically, the rural communities of the fifth century were largely self-sufficient, living on the food from their own fields, making their own pottery for domestic or funerary purposes, and producing within the settlement agricultural implements and the iron toilet-sets so often found with the cremated remains of the dead.

During the fifth century cremation was almost universal among this poor and squalid peasantry in East Anglia, who scratched a bare subsistence from the soil. The dead were placed on the funeral pyre clothed and decked with trinkets such as ivory bracelets or coloured glass beads. The burnt bones and the fused ornaments were placed in bowls or jars, sometimes accompanied by joints of meat for sustenance in the next world. Occasionally the grave-goods suggest that the deceased was wealthy or that he was a 'village character'. Such was the individual whose cremated bones were found at Caistor-by-Norwich with a group of sheep's knuckle-bones, one being inscribed with an unintelligible, and presumably magical, message in Runic, and a set of bone playing-pieces, suggesting that their owner may have been an inveterate gambler. At a few fifth-century cemeteries in Breckland, however, burial was by inhumation, and the associated brooches indicate that these communities are related to other groups in the Cambridge region.

Plate 43

During the century and a half from 500 to 650 many important events occurred in East Anglia. The population was increased by the arrival of fresh invaders, the whole region was brought under the political sway of a single dynasty, and the tenets of Christianity began to be accepted by its pagan inhabitants. The dismal economic uniformity of the fifth century gave place to a society in which differences of wealth were marked and in which, once more, the luxuries of distant lands were supplementing the products of local endeavour.

About 500, further immigrants reached the shores of East Anglia. They can be distinguished from most of the earlier arrivals by their practice of inhumation and by their large square-headed brooches of gilded bronze. From these flashy ornaments it seems that these invaders had come from farther north than the late fourth- and fifth-century Anglo-Saxons, probably from northern Jutland to which they had come from southern Sweden. To call these invaders 'Danes' would only cause confusion in view of the arrival of others bearing the same name in the late ninth century, and it is better to term them the 'Ipswich People' from the large cemetery in that place. From their distinctive brooches and burial rite they can be recognized in the Norwich area at Catton and Brooke, in north-west Norfolk at Hunstanton, and in Breckland at Kenninghall, Mildenhall and Lakenheath, but it is uncertain if these settlements were founded as the result of direct immigration from Denmark, or later colonization from the Sandlings area of south-east Suffolk. It is clear that the newcomers speedily dominated the Suffolk Sandlings, and that this sub-region became the nucleus of the East Anglian kingdom. This is borne out by the later documentary evidence that a royal seat was located in the area at Rendlesham, while the royal cemetery has been discovered at Sutton Hoo near by. The genealogy of the royal family shows that its founder, *c.* 525, was Wehha, whose son Wuffa gave his name to the dynasty. It would seem that Wehha must have been one of the leaders of the Ipswich People when they migrated from Denmark, and he is described by Nennius as the first king 'who reigned in Britain over the East Angles'. We have noted above that the Danes of northern

Jutland, who became our Ipswich People, had reached that area from southern Sweden, and they may possibly be identified with the Geats of *Beowulf*. This colonization took place in the late fifth century and early years of the sixth, and its Swedish derivation is confirmed by the links with that country revealed by the celebrated seventh-century cenotaph of an East Anglian monarch at Sutton Hoo. The contents of this will be described later, but here it is germane to point out its significance in suggesting that the Wuffings, as the East Anglian royal family was known, came from Sweden and were an offshoot of the Scylfings, the royal house of Uppsala, which lies a few miles north of Stockholm. The practice of boat-burial at this time is known only from the Swedish province of Uppland and the Ipswich Zone of East Anglia, and it would be reasonable to derive the latter from the former. Further intimate links between East Anglia and Sweden are provided by the sword, helmet and shield in the Sutton Hoo ship-burial, as these were almost certainly made in Sweden and suggest family heirlooms brought from the mother country in the early sixth century.

Plate 49

Once established in its new home, the Wuffing dynasty lost no time in conquering the whole of East Anglia. The widespread and distinctive cemeteries of the Ipswich People represent the expansion of their power over their neighbours, who were chiefly descended from the Anglo-Saxon-Frisian immigrants of the late fourth and fifth centuries, though other groups can also be detected. The Breckland communities who inhumed their dead have already been mentioned, and small pockets of other foreigners are suggested by the place-names Shotesham and Scottow in Norfolk, indicating the presence of Scots from Ireland, and by a remarkable antler knife-handle from Weeting in south-west Norfolk inscribed unintelligibly in Ogham and suggesting a Pictish mercenary far from his homeland in northern Scotland. Wuffing domination over these diverse communities was probably achieved by *c.* 550. By the end of the

Plate 44

century their power and cultural influence had reached as far as the Nene valley, and the apogee of the East Anglian king, dom was attained under the rule of Raedwald, who succeeded to the throne *c.* 599. His military and political supremacy was such that, for a brief period from *c.* 610 until his death in 624–5, he was acknowledged overlord of southern England. His successors were not of similar calibre and proved unable to resist the rising strength of the kingdoms of Northumbria and Mercia. Within the generation following Raedwald's death, no less than four East Anglian kings fell in battle vainly attempting to prevent their realm falling under the political control of these larger states. Henceforth, East Anglia was merely a satellite of its more powerful neighbours and its monarchs puppet kings.

The place-name 'Eccles', which occurs twice in Norfolk, may indicate a survival of Late Roman Christianity into the Early Saxon Age, but this cannot have endured for long, as the whole area was clearly pagan until the early years of the seventh century. Before 617 Raedwald became converted to Christianity, perhaps for political reasons while on a visit to the King of Kent, an area which had been Christian since the mission of St Augustine in 597. On his return he set up an altar for Christian worship in his temple, perhaps at Rendlesham, but, as Bede relates, on the advice of his pagan wife 'and certain false teachers' retained in the same temple 'another little altar for offerings made to devils'. Raedwald was succeeded by his son, Eorpwald, who *c.* 628 was persuaded by King Edwin of Northumbria 'to leave off the superstitions of idols, and with his whole realm receive the faith and sacraments of Christ'. Eorpwald's conversion may have led to his murder in 628 when a pagan usurper seized power for two or three years until Eorpwald's Christian half-brother Sigeberht returned from exile in Gaul to mount the throne of the East Angles. One of his first acts was to seek the aid of Archbishop Honorius at Canterbury in preaching the Gospel. Honorius sent to him

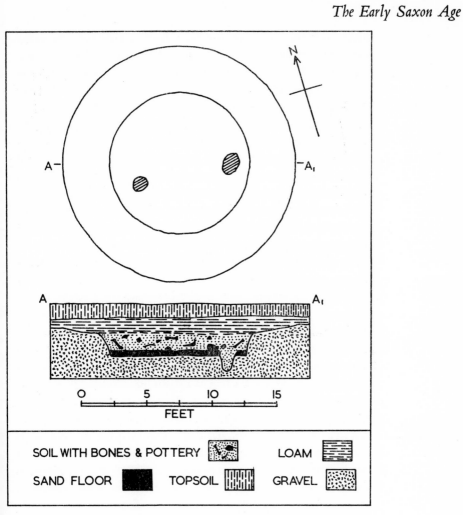

Fig. 33 Plan and section of hut-site. Pakenham, Suffolk

Bishop Felix from Burgundy, who established a missionary base at Dunwich and soon converted the kingdom. About 636 Sigeberht was visited by an eminent ascetic, St Fursey, who had come direct from Ireland, and who was allowed to establish a monastery inside the ruined Roman fortress at Burgh Castle, where the post-holes and painted wall-plaster of some of its buildings have recently been found. Other monasteries, also of timber construction, were soon founded at Blythburgh, Bury and *Icanhoh* (probably Iken), whose abbot, Botulf, became celebrated as a model monastic saint. Unlike their brethren in other parts of the country the Christians of East Anglia appear to have lived in concord, despite their mixed Irish and continental origins.

Fig. 33

In recent years, a few hut-sites of the sixth and early seventh centuries have been recognized or excavated at Butley, Freckenham, Mildenhall and Pakenham in Suffolk, and at Postwick, Snettisham and Thetford in Norfolk. In plan, these are round, oval or sub-rectangular, not more than 15 feet across and generally dug into the ground to a depth of one or two feet. It is probable that the walls were of wattle-and-daub and that the roof of thatch rested on a ridge-pole supported on upright posts. It has been suggested that these squalid huts were only for cooking or weaving, but the accumulation on the floors of broken pottery, spindle whorls, discarded animal bones and filth may as well have resulted from permanent habitation. As in the fifth century, no traces have yet been found of either large farmhouses or aristocratic timber-halls of the type described in *Beowulf*, but this apparent absence is doubtless due to faulty archaeology. From our present knowledge of habitations we should infer that the whole population consisted of poverty-stricken peasants, but the evidence of burials belies this.

Fig. 34

The population buried in the village cemeteries of the sixth and early seventh centuries probably consisted mainly of slaves and churls or ordinary freemen. Those communities, chiefly of Angle origin, which had been accustomed to cremate their dead in the fifth century continued to do so until the middle of the seventh, as the Lackford cemetery shows. Other groups practised in' humation, especially the Ipswich People whose dominant role in the formation of the kingdom of East Anglia led to the spread of this burial rite. These inhumation graves show that the pagan Anglo'Saxon was buried in clothes, ranging from the texture of a flannel shirt to that of tweed. The bodies of men are often accompanied by spears, knives and round shields, while

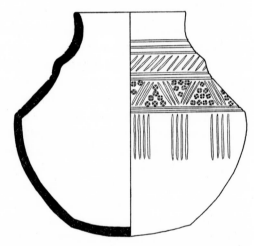

Fig. 34   Cremation urn from cemetery. North Elmham, Norfolk. Scale ¼

those of women were usually buried with bead necklaces, brooches, bracelets and keys; many were supplied with food. Though most of the deceased were placed in urn cemeteries or flat gravefields, some bodies were inserted in prehistoric barrows or covered by freshly constructed mounds, as, for instance, at Northwold and Sporle in Norfolk. One of the barrows at the latter site covered seven warriors who had been laid to rest in woollen cloaks and covered by round shields. In addition to covering multiple inhumations and cremations such as those on

Brightwell Heath, Suffolk, barrows are particularly associated with aristocratic inhumation burials of the Ipswich People, who probably re-introduced barrow burial into East Anglia. One of their chieftains, found in a barrow at Pakefield, near Lowestoft, was decked with jewellery including a gold coin pendant and a necklet of rough garnets, and had been buried in the early seventh century. An even more remarkable discovery was made at Snape, where, between *c.* 635 and 650, another chieftain was placed beneath a barrow in a 50-foot boat. Though the grave had been looted, when excavated it still contained a magnificent gold finger-ring inset with a gem, and glass vessels. The significance of boat-burial has already been noted in assessing the Scandinavian origins of the monarchy of the Ipswich People, and it is appropriate to end this section with a brief account of the ship-burial in the Sutton Hoo barrow group eight miles south of Snape. At the time of its discovery in 1939 it was suggested that 'there are few who will dispute that the Sutton Hoo ship-burial may well prove to be the most significant, as it is certainly the most splendid, archaeological discovery ever made in the British Isles'. Since then, detailed technical and comparative studies have been made, but the last word has not yet been said, and will not be until the remainder of this cemetery has been adequately excavated. A bare list of the contents of this ship-barrow containing 'the first royal grave of this era in Europe to have come down to modern times un-burnt and unrobbed' would occupy many pages.

The royal cemetery consists of at least ten barrows over-looking the east bank of the Deben, and would have been visible to shipping in this busy estuary, which joins the sea six miles away. The ship-barrow was an oval mound formerly at least 12 feet high and over 100 feet long, covering a great open rowing vessel, 86 feet long, which had been dragged into a deep trench. It was built for a crew of 38 oarsmen. The incredibly rich grave-goods lay in a gabled cabin, about 10 feet high,

Plate 48

situated amidships. We are faced with the difficulty that it contained no body and never had done so; that in fact it was a cenotaph to a powerful and wealthy Christian king of Scandinavian antecedents, buried elsewhere but commemorated in the pagan heroic tradition in a pagan cemetery. The most likely candidate for this honour is Anna, a revered Christian king who died in 654 attempting to repel an invasion of East Anglia by the pagan Penda of Mercia. Alternatively, the barrow and its contents may be a memorial to Anna's brother, Aethelhere, who perished in the following year in the floodwaters at the battle of Winwaed in Yorkshire. Whichever may be the case, on the evidence of the hoard of Merovingian gold coins it contained there can be no doubt that the memorial was erected between 650 and 670. The royal status of the individual commemorated is established by the presence of a wrought-iron standard of authority, by a giant whetstone or sceptre and by the immense wealth represented by the golden harness and other treasures. This gold equipment, consisting of forty-one objects of solid gold, heavily encrusted with garnets and including a belt-buckle, hinged shoulder-clasps, mounts for suspending a sword, and a purse-lid, is made with great technical skill and artistic feeling. It has been described as 'the finest Dark Age jewellery of its class in Europe', and was almost certainly made in Suffolk in the early seventh century by a master goldsmith in service at the East Anglian court. The military qualities of the monarchy are emphasized not only by the Scandinavian heir-looms—the sword (with its Rhenish pattern-welded blade), the shield and the helmet—but also by more up-to-date warlike equipment such as the coat of mail, knife, axe, throwing javelins and spears. The lavish entertainment and revelry of feasting in the royal hall are vividly suggested by the remains of a six-stringed harp (in its beaver-skin bag), drinking horns with silver-gilt mounts—two being from the horns of the aurochs and holding six quarts of mead or ale apiece—and tiny gourds

Plate 45

Plate 47

Plate 49

with similar mounts for stronger liquor. Other items of equipment are iron-bound wooden buckets, sheet-bronze cauldrons,
a heavy bronze bowl decorated with lion, tiger and camel (made
in Alexandria), bronze hanging-bowls from western England
or Ireland, and silver dishes and bowls made in the Byzantine
Empire. One large, silver salver bore the control stamp of
Anastasius I (491–518). A pair of late classical silver spoons,
inscribed 'Saulos' and 'Paulos', were doubtless a baptismal
present for a Christian convert. There were also items of
domestic and personal equipment, such as iron chainwork for
the suspension of cauldrons, a pottery bottle, wooden cups or
bowls, remains of combs, textiles, leather slippers and a leather
bag, silver shoe-buckles and a pillow stuffed with goose down.
So comprehensive a list sounds fantastic, and is eloquent of the
wealth of the dynasty which was able to collect treasures from
such distant sources. Other chance finds from elsewhere in East
Anglia also testify to the luxury goods which the wealth and
the sea-power of the Wuffings brought to its harbours and
diffused among its aristocracy.

By the mid sixth century the old self-sufficiency was breaking
down, and the domestic and funerary pottery produced by the
women of the village was being supplemented by the products
of itinerant professional potters, though still without the aid of a
wheel. These can be recognized by their similarity in form and
fabric and by the use of identical stamps; the wares of the same
potter have, for instance, been identified in the cemeteries of
Lackford and Illington, nearly twenty miles apart. During the
late sixth century considerable influence from Middle Anglia is
apparent on pottery found in East Anglia. By the early seventh
century East Anglia began to feel the effects of the cultural
expansion of Kent, and fine examples of jewellery of Kentish
type are found not only in the Ipswich region and in Breckland,
but even in north-east Norfolk, where a gold coin-pendant,
once set around with garnets, was found on the beach at Bacton.

Plate 46

Foreign products appeared only rarely in our area in the fifth and sixth centuries and all demonstrate trade with the Rhineland. This supplied bowls and beakers of glass, and cauldrons, brooches and buckles of bronze. It was only after *c.* 600 that continental trade developed on a more extensive scale, when Rhenish glassware reached the Ipswich region in larger quantities, though it was never so common there as in south-east England. This trade with the Rhineland was probably responsible for the appearance of oriental luxuries at Sutton Hoo, Caistor-by-Norwich and Wickham Market, Suffolk, probably all from aristocratic graves.

The third and last phase of the Early Saxon Age, from *c.* 650 to 850, witnessed the decline of the political power of the East Anglian kingdom, the apparent triumph of Christianity over heathenism and a considerable growth in the population of the area. The terminal date of 850 forms a convenient point of division between the Early and Late Saxon Ages, when the Danish raids suddenly expanded into large-scale invasion and subsequent settlement.

Throughout this phase, East Anglia remained a separate kingdom though its monarchs were politically subject to the more powerful states which were evolving from smaller units. It came in turn under the suzerainty of Northumbria (to 658), of Mercia and finally, from 829, of Wessex. The Wuffing dynasty came to an end in the person of Aelfwald, who died *c.* 740. During the next century the names of eight kings are recorded, but little is known of them; in some cases their order of accession is obscure and their regnal dates are guesswork. The fate of vassal kings who attempted to assert their independence is well shown by Ethelbert, who was beheaded in 794 at Sutton Walls, near Hereford, by the orders of Offa of Mercia. In terms of power politics the East Anglian monarchy had sunk far since the days of Raedwald, yet the sheer facts of geography and the difficulty distant overlords had in exercising effective control must have meant a considerable measure of internal self-government for East Anglia.

The intimate links between the personality of the monarch and the diffusion of Christian ideas have already been noticed. The continued fostering of the new faith by the East Anglian kings is apparent in the late seventh and eighth centuries. No less than four daughters of King Anna served as abbess of a monastery or as a member of a religious community. King Aelfwald not only carried on a correspondence with St Boniface, who led an Anglo-Saxon mission to Germany, but also ordered the compilation of a life of St Guthlac, the founder of Crowland Abbey. The mission headquarters of St Felix at Dunwich remained the centre of a see which probably covered the whole of East Anglia, but the difficulties of geo-graphy and the needs of an expanding population led to the division of the diocese in 673, when a separate see was established with headquarters at North Elmham. The selection of this site was probably due to its central position in this new see for Norfolk. No trace of any ecclesiastical buildings of this period has yet been found at North Elmham, doubtless because they were constructed of timber and daub. The local monasteries erected in the first flush of Christianity would have been built of similar materials, and in the absence of excavation it cannot be known if they were double monasteries for men and women of the type founded at Ely in 673. The spread of monasticism brought with it literacy and a devotion to scholarship for which the Anglo-Saxon church became justly famous. Later destruc-tion has deprived us of most of the books of these early monasteries, a seventh-century whalebone writing-tablet from the monastery at Blythburgh being the sole survivor from the area with which we are concerned.

Graveyards were probably established adjacent to the newly founded monasteries and churches, but the process must have been slow and some Christians and obstinate pagans were doubtless interred in their traditional cemeteries until the latter part of the seventh century. Bodies were laid facing the eastern quarter and some were still accompanied by grave-goods, though this became increasingly rare. Many cemeteries begun in this period have continued in use until the present day; this, together with the normal absence of grave-goods, makes the dating of any individual interment extraordinarily difficult. Some cemeteries, however, were subsequently abandoned, and a few of these have recently been investigated. At Caister-by-Yarmouth over 150 burials, from between *c.* 650 and 850, have been excavated outside the ditches of the Roman town, and others occurred inside the walled area. The most remarkable discovery here was of about a dozen graves, dating from the late seventh century, which had not been filled with earth but covered with timbers from a ship's side, of which the iron clench nails survive. These 'pseudo ship-burials' would appear to be a poor man's version of the pagan tradition embodied in the Sutton Hoo cenotaph and imply the derivation of the Caister community from the Ipswich region. In the lower levels of a churchyard within the later Red Castle at Thetford, isolated human skulls, presumably decapitated, were found buried inside a nest of flints and this practice may well be a pagan survival into the eighth or ninth century.

Plate 50
Fig. 30

Students of place-names are agreed that those now ending in -*ing* and -*ingham* are among the most archaic English names in this country. Together with the name of the leader of a small group of people (e.g. Docking, formerly *Doccingas*—the people or followers of *Docca*), they are common in East Anglia, over eighty being known in Norfolk alone. We cannot be sure that these are the names of settlements or farms undoubtedly founded in the fifth or sixth centuries; from most of the parishes in question no archaeological finds of this period are recorded, but when any is known it ranges indiscriminately from the fifth, the sixth or the seventh century. It is unlikely on philological grounds that these names can have been given later than the end of the seventh century, and they therefore indicate a larger population by that time than we had previously de-duced from archaeological evidence alone. It would be unwise to assume that archaeological material discovered within a modern parish bearing one of these names was necessarily associated with that group of people, for doubtless many Early Saxon Age settlements perished in the Danish raids of the ninth century, never to be rebuilt, so that their names did not survive for incorporation in the Domesday record. These *-ing* and *-ingham* names are commonest in central, south and north-east Norfolk and in south-east Suffolk, and appear to represent the first stages in the Anglo-Saxon colonization of the heavier soils, hitherto under forest, by a young and vigorous population whose average age at death was only thirty. Whether this develop-ment was due to further immigration from overseas or to local expansion from earlier settlements must remain uncertain until more archaeological evidence is available.

Little is known about the structural features of houses in East Anglia between *c.* 650 and 850, and still less about the lay-out of villages. At Caister-by-Yarmouth the huts scattered inside the ruins of the Roman town were oval or round, one being 16½ feet in diameter, while at Sedgeford both round and rectangular houses have been found, though it is uncertain if these are strictly contemporaneous. Indications of sleeper beams at West Stow in north-west Suffolk also suggest the existence of rectangular timber-framed houses.

As in preceding centuries the economy of East Anglia from the seventh to the ninth century was basically agricultural, though little is known of its system of land-holding. Evidence from other districts suggests a social structure of a few noble-men, many churls or freemen and numerous slaves. There is no proof that the open-field system, common in the Midlands and southern England, existed in East Anglia and little to show what took its place. We may perhaps assume that its principal crops were wheat or barley, supplemented by beans, peas and flax.

Although farming was the mainstay of the population, the first feeble traces of town life since Roman times may be detected before the end of the Early Saxon Age. Sudbury is mentioned in the Anglo-Saxon Chronicle in 798, and its name *Suthbyrig* (Southern Burg) suggests a township though no confirmatory archaeological evidence is yet known. Future discoveries may well show that a township existed at Norwich as early as this,

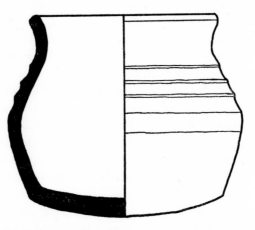

Fig. 35   Cooking-pot of Ipswich (Middle Saxon) ware. Ipswich, Suffolk. Scale ½

but it is only at Ipswich that there is good evidence for the existence of a trading centre in the late seventh or early eighth century. This conclusion is deduced from the discovery there of kilns for firing pottery made on a slow wheel (Ipswich ware), sometimes in a harsh pimply ware, sometimes in a smoother fabric. Until this Middle Saxon pottery was fashioned, no wheel-made pottery had been produced in England for over two centuries. It seems likely that the use of the wheel and of kilns was introduced *c.* 650 to the Ipswich area by immigrant potters from the Rhineland, perhaps through the commercial

Fig. 35

contacts of Frisian merchants. Once the basic ideas had been introduced, the industry was developed by local personnel. The diffusion of Ipswich ware indicates the economic dominance of the Ipswich region at this time, and the mainly coastal distribution of this ware suggests coast-wise trading. Politically, East Anglia may have been a satellite kingdom, but its close links with the continent gave it considerable economic power and an industrial technique in advance of the rest of England. The activities of Frisian merchants in the carrying trade were probably responsible for such imports as the Frankish bronze mount for a woman's purse found in the cemetery at Framling-ham, and the eighth- or early ninth-century pot from the kilns at Badorf on the Rhine of which a fragment was found in Ipswich in 1957. The stimulus of this trade led to the minting of small silver coins called *sceattas*, of which the East Anglian types seem to date from the early eighth century. Examples of these and other English types are widely diffused in Frisia and indicate the extent of this intercourse. Silver pennies were first issued by Offa of Mercia about 775, and *sceattas* gave way to this new currency. The first inscribed coins that can be attributed to a specific East Anglian monarch are those bearing the name of Athelstan I, who reigned *c.* 825–840, and of his successor Ethelweard. Throughout the eighth and early ninth centuries the political and economic ties with the other English kingdoms led to the introduction of the coins of Kent, Mercia and Wessex. The final absorption of East Anglia by Wessex is fittingly symbolized by a Canterbury penny, minted for Ecgbeorht of Wessex *c.* 830 and found beneath the head of a body in the Caister-by-Yarmouth cemetery. In a few years East Anglia was to face a peril beside which its forcible annexation by another English kingdom was to appear like a friendly embrace.

CHAPTER IX

The Late Saxon Age

THE TWO CENTURIES of the Late Saxon Age (850–1066) are among the most significant in the long history of East Anglia. Despite the cataclysm of the Danish invasions, this period saw the creation of the basic economy of Medieval and modern East Anglia. By the Norman Conquest of 1066, Norfolk and Suffolk had developed into two of the wealthiest and most populous counties in England, with prosperous towns, flourishing industry, a dense rural population and a vigorous church life. This economic expansion was achieved in a kingdom torn by the fury of the Danish invaders, with consequent loss of life, devastation of property, destruction of church treasures and the temporary submergence of organized Christianity. The thoroughness of the Danish attacks, with historical records perishing in the flames, has deprived us of the documents which might have illumined this economic miracle, and information from surviving chronicles and charters is tantalizingly meagre. Formerly, archaeological evidence for Late Saxon East Anglia was almost entirely restricted to ecclesiastical remains of the eleventh century, but the recognition of Late Saxon pottery and the extensive excavations at Thetford, now the best explored Saxon town site in Britain, have transformed the situation.

Invasions of East Anglia by Danes spanned the Late Saxon Age, the first recorded raid on the region taking place in 841 and final fruitless attacks on Ipswich and Norwich occurring in 1069. These part-time adventurers, under their well-born leaders, after fighting and plundering one another turned their attention to the neighbouring Christian kingdoms, partly from economic and partly from political motives. The success of their attacks was due to a variety of factors. As individuals they were tough, enterprising and ruthlessly cruel; as a group they displayed remarkable qualities of discipline which welded them into a formidable fighting organization. Their technical skill in building ships, now equipped with sails as well as oars, and their superb seamanship enabled them to under-take long voyages—even across the North Atlantic—and gave them great mobility in their raiding. Once ashore, they normally seized horses, not for fighting as cavalry but for rapid transport to their chosen target or battlefield, thus frequently out-manœuvring the slow-moving Anglo-Saxon levies. Sporadic raids, like that of 841, gave place in 865 to a large-scale landing in East Anglia, then the smallest and weakest of the English kingdoms. The arrival of this 'Great Heathen Army' under the control of Ivar the Boneless and his brother marks the first stage in the Danish conquest of eastern England. For thirteen years the 'Great Army' marched and counter-marched across England, until at length mutual exhaustion led to a temporary settlement. The size of the 'Great Army' is unknown, but on occasion it must have comprised several thousand men. It was provided with horses as part of the terms imposed on the East Anglian population in 865, when the Danes first established their winter quarters among them. The next spring the army went north to attack York, and after ravaging Mercia returned to East Anglia in the autumn of 869 and set up winter quarters at Thetford, possibly the earliest occupation over much of this site. At about the same time, using to the full the mobility conferred by sea-power, another group of the invaders arrived 'suddenly with a great fleet, landed by stealth at a city in that region (possibly Norwich), entered it before the citizens were aware . . . and set it on fire'. The precise sequence of military movements at this time is obscure, but it is clear that King Edmund of the East Angles

Fig. 36

fought with one or possibly both of these invading forces, was captured, tortured by archers while bound to a tree, and finally

Fig. 36   Late Saxon drawing of martyrdom of St Edmund

beheaded. Several early accounts place the martyrdom of the king at a locality usually rendered 'Haegelisdun' and now identifiable with Hellesdon on the western outskirts of Norwich. His execution here would have been doubly effective if this was the most important township in his realm. Later legends relate that King Edmund's body was recovered and buried at Hoxne, but earlier records state that he was interred at Sutton, perhaps a significant and defiant re-use of the old East Anglian royal cemetery of Sutton Hoo.

In the spring of 870 the 'Great Army' moved from its quarters at Thetford and advanced down the Icknield Way to an all-out assault on Wessex, leaving East Anglia for the next half century under effective Danish control. As else-where, this involved the murder of many East Anglian notables, both lay and spiritual, the defilement and destruction of churches and monasteries and the enslavement of the population. By 878 Guthrum, now the chief leader of the Danish army, was still bent on the destruction of the kingdom of Wessex, which alone stood between him and the mastery of Southern England. He successfully attacked the forces of King Alfred, but within a few weeks, the tables were turned at the decisive battle of Ethandun in Wiltshire, and Guthrum was forced to accept the treaty of Chippenham. By this compact the Danes agreed to leave Wessex and Guthrum to accept Christianity with King Alfred as his godfather. It was presumably also part of the agreement that Guthrum, in the following year, marched back to East Anglia and 'occupied that land and shared it out'. Some indications of the area settled by the soldiers of Guthrum's army are provided by the survival of Danish place-names. Names terminating in -by (implying a village), associated with *thorpe* (a subsidiary farm), *toft* (a house), *thwaite* (a clearing), or compounded with Scandinavian personal names, some 200 in all, are good evidence for the extent of the settlement begun in 879. From this distribution it is clear that most of the

Fig. 37

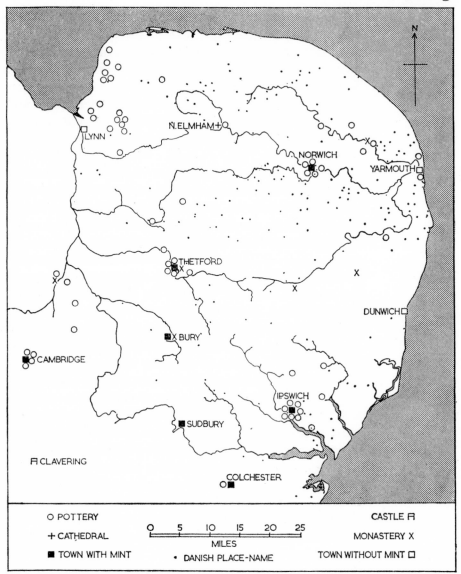

Fig. 37   Distribution of Late Saxon culture and Danish place-names

lands allotted to the Danish soldiers were in the eastern parts of Norfolk and Suffolk. Part of this area, like the island of Flegg, north of Yarmouth, had only been sparsely occupied up to this time, but elsewhere in Norfolk and Suffolk the distribution of parish names suggests that some Anglo-Saxons were evicted and their lands handed over to Danes. It was presumably Alfred's policy that this area of concentrated Danish settlement should be isolated from that in the East Midlands by the Anglo-Saxon area of west Norfolk, north-west Suffolk and Cambridgeshire. His anticipation of further conflict with the East Anglian Danes was amply justified, for in 884 he had to send a naval force to the mouth of the Stour, where it routed a Danish fleet. In the following year 'the host in East Anglia broke peace with King Alfred', as the Anglo-Saxon Chronicle laconically describes the outbreak of hostilities. This was ended by a fresh treaty between Guthrum and Alfred, who now felt that he represented the whole of the English nation outside Danish control, instead of merely the kingdom of Wessex. This agreement defined the boundary of Guthrum's kingdom 'Greater East Anglia' as from the mouth of the Thames, along the rivers Lea and Ouse to Watling Street, and so included, in addition to the original East Anglian kingdom of Norfolk and Suffolk, the adjacent counties of Essex, Cambridgeshire and Huntingdonshire with parts of Bedfordshire and Hertford-shire. Outside 'Greater East Anglia', the Danes were also in control of the East Midlands and Northumbria; the Danelaw thus stretched from the mouth of the Thames to the mouth of the Mersey. It was Alfred's intention that his boundary with the Danelaw should be an iron curtain to be traversed as infre-quently as possible, but his plans were soon frustrated.

In 879 some of the 'Great Army' had gone overseas to Belgium and France to continue their piratical activities. Baffled by mounting opposition in those countries, they returned after 892 to attack England and were vigorously supported by East Anglian Danes raiding from across their frontier. After four years this war petered out and the main problem which then faced Alfred and his successor, Edward, was the reconquest of the Danelaw. Raids such as the ravaging of west Norfolk by Edward preceded a slow war of attrition in which Anglo-Saxon gains were consolidated by the construction of *burgs* or forts. Some of these were doubtless earlier fortifications reconditioned, but others were new constructions. Archaeologically, none of the newly constructed *burgs* have yet been identified in East Anglia, but some at least of the place-names containing the element *burh* or *burg*, such as Burgh St Margaret and Aldborough in Norfolk, may indicate their sites. At all events, the distribution of *burg* place-names in eastern East Anglia approximates to that of Danish place-names and may thus indicate the measures taken for holding down the Danes after the reconquest was completed about 920.

This apparent failure of the archaeological evidence to support reasonable historical deductions is also true of the whole phase of the Danish invasions. The archaeological material as yet known consists of little more than one early tenth-century Danish burial, a few stirrups and fragmentary weapons recovered from rivers; nothing in fact to suggest more than the arrival of a few Danes and some sporadic fighting, and yet the historical record is clear and unmistakable.

Plates 52, 53

After its reconquest in 920, Anglo-Danish East Anglia became part of a united England, and this integration is illustrated by the coins in the great hoard found at Morley St Peter, Norfolk, in 1958. The bulk of these bear the effigy of Edward the Elder, and had been produced by his moneyers sent from southern England to set up a new mint in this reconquered territory, almost certainly at Norwich. For the next two generations there are clear indications in both town and country of peace and prosperity, with Anglo-Saxons and Danes forming a community of interest to such effect that, when Danish

Fig. 38

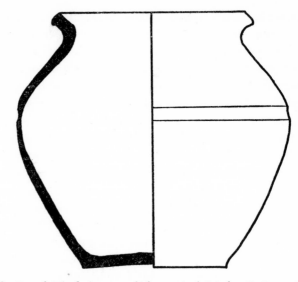

Fig. 38   Jar of Thetford ware which contained Morley St Peter, Norfolk, coin hoard, concealed c. *925. Scale* ½

attacks began again towards the end of the tenth century, most East Anglians regarded themselves as Englishmen. Raiding had been resumed soon after the accession of the weak King Aethelred II in 979, and in 991 Ipswich was attacked from the sea by a force of about 5,000 men, who turned south into Essex and fought the battle of Maldon. In this same year the English began a policy of appeasement by paying ten thousand pounds by weight to the Danes (Danegeld) 'because of the great terror they inspired along the sea coast'. But this political degeneracy and the inept massacre of St Brice's Day in 1002 only led to further trouble. Two years later, massive retaliation began when Swein Forkbeard, King of Denmark, led a highly skilled and disciplined professional army to Norwich from military bases in Denmark. Swein sacked Norwich and burned it and, for the moment, the unprepared East Anglians under Ulfcytel Snilling bought peace. Under cover of this truce, the Danes moved secretly from Norwich towards Thetford. When Ulfcytel discovered this he sent agents to destroy the Danish fleet, but the plan miscarried. Swein reached Thetford and his forces pillaged and burned it. Next morning Ulfcytel with a scratch force attacked the Danes and many prominent East Anglians, as well as Danes, fell in the battle. The Danes retired to their fleet admitting 'that they had never met with harder handplay in England than Ulfcytel gave them'. This tough warrior was ready for them when the next invasion took place in 1010. The Danes under Thorkell the Tall landed at Ipswich, and went straight to where Ulfcytel awaited them. This was at Ringmere Heath in East Wretham or at Rymer, south of Thetford, and there the last great battle in East Anglia between English and Dane was fought. The East Anglian levies (possibly mainly of Danish extraction) soon broke, but the Anglo-Saxons of Cambridgeshire held their ground, yet were powerless to prevent a Danish victory; many were slaughtered including the king's son-in-law—'Hringmara heath was a bed of death'. For three months the Danes then harried East Anglia, burning Thetford and Cambridge, 'even penetrating into the uninhabited fens, slaying men and cattle, and burning throughout the fens', before they turned southwards. This devastating attack, followed by others of even greater intensity on the whole of eastern and south-eastern England, brought the English government to its knees. London surrendered, Aethelred fled to Normandy and Swein was acknowledged as king of England. Swein and Aethelred died in quick succession, and after a brief interval with English and Danish kings ruling different areas, the whole of England from 1016 to 1042 fell under Danish rule, first of Cnut, son of Swein, and then of Cnut's two sons. The prolonged absences of Cnut in Scandinavia, where, for a time, he added Norway to his empire, led to the delegation of administrative responsibility in England and to the division of the country among powerful magnates. In 1017 Thorkell the Tall was given charge of the earldom of East Anglia, the area of which varied from time to time but approximated to the old Danish kingdom held by Guthrum, though for a few years it included, in addition, Oxfordshire. During the reign of Edward the Confessor the East Anglian earldom was held by Harold, who was to become the last Anglo-Saxon king, and by his brother, Gyrth, both sons of the powerful Godwine. Harold and Gyrth both fell on the field of Hastings resisting the Norman attack in 1066, and with them perished the Anglo-Danish state.

The summary we have given of warfare and political activities in East Anglia may have produced the impression that this period was dominated by destruction, and marked by economic retardation. Yet this impression would be false. Destruction there undoubtedly was—towns, villages and farms were pillaged and burned; churches and monasteries were obliterated; king, bishop, nobles and rank and file fell on the field of battle or at the hands of an execution squad; the learning and culture of the seventh and eighth centuries were ruined—yet economically it was a period of amazing advance. The combined evidence of archaeology and place-names suggests a small and scattered population before 850; but by 1066, on the testimony of Domesday Book, East Anglia supported an infinitely larger population than ever before, and must be reckoned as one of the most densely peopled regions in Britain. In Norfolk and Suffolk a minimum of sixty thousand persons may safely be assumed, and the real number is likely to have been four or five times greater. They dwelt in at least one thousand, three hundred and sixty-five taxable localities in the two counties, and the majority of these must have been established in the two centuries before the Norman Conquest, for very few settlements of the sixth or the seventh centuries seem to have survived into Late Saxon and Early Medieval times. The fate of these earlier settlements is uncertain. Some may have been abandoned at the conversion to Christianity, others were moved to new sites for economic reasons, and yet others were destroyed by the Danish onslaughts. At Caister-by-Yarmouth the village established *c.* 650 was probably compulsorily abandoned when Danish settlement began in the area after 879. Behind the dull statistics of Domesday we must envisage not only the arrival of a few thousand Danes, but a significant expansion of the Anglo-Saxon population. The creation of farms and villages by the Danes and the Anglo-Saxons must have led to large-scale deforestation in Flegg, in the district south and east of Norwich and in the wooded clay country generally. This vigorous pioneering with felling axe and fire, this carving of arable and pasture out of woodland and scrub, this erection of houses and churches and creation of roads and tracks, all serve to indicate the determination of an expanding population to dominate its surroundings and wrest a living from the more fertile soils of East Anglia; so that by Domesday there was a dense population evenly distributed over the region. One highly significant result of this expansion, with exploitation of the richer soils in Mid and east Norfolk and to a lesser extent in Suffolk, was that the economic centre moved eastwards from the Breckland Zone, in which it had been located since Neolithic times, to the Norwich area and to the Ipswich region. The growth of Norwich and Ipswich from the late ninth century symbolizes this shift of economic power.

We know singularly little about the rural economy of East Anglia before the compilation of the Domesday record but it seems clear that open-fields of the type familiar in the Mid-lands were never common. The arable land was probably held in compact holdings which were gradually broken up by division among co-heirs. Large numbers of livestock were kept; Domesday records nearly 84,000 sheep in the two counties, nearly 18,000 swine and over 7,000 goats. The cultivation of the heavy clay soils depended on draught oxen of two main types, the long-horned red cattle best represented today by the Hereford breed, and the polled red cattle from which the Suffolk Dun is descended. Inland fisheries were also of considerable economic importance, particularly round the eastern margins of Fenland, and doubtless there was some sea fishing as well. The annual slaughter of beasts, necessitated by the lack of winter feed, produced a steady demand for large quantities of salt for the preservation of the meat. This salt was obtained by the evapora- tion of brine in salt-pans and many of these are recorded in Domesday, particularly on the eastern shore of the Wash, round the estuary of the Stour and in the 'Great Estuary' behind Yarmouth. Farther up the valleys of the rivers that flow out at Yarmouth we may be reasonably certain, despite the silence of Domesday on this point, that for most of the Late Saxon Age men had been digging deep pits for the extraction of peat for fuel. Though supplies of timber had been diminished by the encroachments of agriculture, industry and building, consider- able woods still survived to provide acorns and beechmast for swine. However, the growing shortage of wood may have stimulated the population to use peat as an alternative fuel, an idea which may well have been introduced by the Danes who came from a land of peat-bogs.

It has been suggested that the Danish element was repre- sented by the large numbers of free peasants who appear in the Domesday record, those in East Anglia forming the largest concentration of this group of the community to be found in eleventh-century England. It is true that the concentrations of free peasants coincide roughly with the areas of intense Danish settlement and that the main aggregation of serfs (in Breckland) lies in an area with few Danish villages; yet the true explanation is probably different. With the growth of powerful hereditary magnates in the tenth and eleventh centuries, many smaller landowners, particularly those scratching a bare existence from the poorer soils, voluntarily commended themselves to richer lords, economically and legally, in order to survive. The free peasantry of Domesday seem then to be survivors of a once more widespread class, who had managed to retain their economic independence because they dwelt on richer lands or were more efficient cultivators. Their less fortunate brethren were already becoming manorialized. Very little is known about the local administration of East Anglia in the Late Saxon Age, but it seems that the Hundred (there were over fifty of these in the area) was, from the tenth century, the unit of local government, and that the principal function of its court was to round up stray cattle and bring thieves to judgment. Above the Hundred was the county organization, but the antiquity of this is obscure. Suffolk is first mentioned in 895 (*Pagus Suthfolchi*—the South Folk) and though Norfolk does not appear in any surviving record before 1043–5, it may be assumed to be at least as old. It would appear unlikely that the counties of East Anglia were created by the Danes, as it seems probable that their areas are related to the areas of the dioceses of Dunwich and Elmham defined in 673. Is it rash to deduce that our counties are as old as that and reflect the different origins of the Ipswich People (the South Folk) on the one hand, and the predominantly Angle population of Norfolk (the North Folk) on the other?

At the close of the last chapter we drew attention to the growth of permanent trading centres in the eighth and early ninth centuries, but the townships which existed by 850 at Ipswich, Sudbury, Norwich, and perhaps elsewhere, were extremely small and by modern standards would only be rated as villages. By 1066, at least eight towns can be recognized in Norfolk and Suffolk with populations of up to 5,000, most of whom were engaged in trade or industry. Despite the repeated ravaging of these towns by the Danes, there can be little doubt that the real expansion from trading village to urban community is due to the settlement there of these invaders

in the late ninth century. The merchant's need for security w
engaged in commerce and the economic requirements of
royal treasury both led to the concentration of markets
few towns where effective control could be exercised.
emergence of urban communities and their subsequent grc
was a result of an increasingly prosperous rural econc
created by the exploitation of the richer soils following f
clearance. Flourishing commerce required a uniform curre
and in the tenth century it was enacted that there should be
one currency throughout the realm, though the privileg
striking coins was granted to a number of towns. During
Late Saxon Age coins were struck at Norwich, Ipsw
Thetford, Sudbury and Bury St Edmunds, and the dat
which this privilege was granted and the number of mon
operating provides some indication of the relative econc
status of these towns; from various entries in the Dome
record it is possible to form a very rough estimate of their
With approximately 5,000 inhabitants at the Nor
Conquest, Norwich was clearly the most populous, follo
closely by Thetford with between 4,000 and 5,000. Dun
and Bury may have boasted about 3,000 each and Ipswich
at least 1,300 and probably many more. Lynn, Yarmouth
Sudbury were much smaller, with populations of about
It is uncertain if these towns were fortified, but the con
threat of warfare would suggest that they were. The
discovery in 1959 of the eleventh-century town ditche
Thetford and Ipswich points to the likelihood of similar defe
at other towns. In the space at our disposal some account
be given of only the two largest, Norwich and Thetford.

The archaeological evidence for the early settlemen
Norwich is sealed beneath modern buildings, and even w
some investigation has been possible, it is found that repe
rebuilding of the city in Medieval times, a consequence c
great wealth, has destroyed much of the evidence of ea

Fig. 39

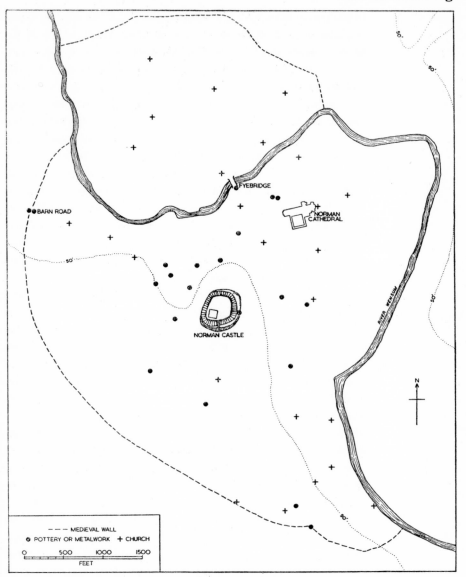

Fig. 39   Plan of Norwich showing distribution of Saxo-Norman remains

occupation. The first documentary evidence for the existence of a township at Norwich consists of the record of its destruction in 1004, but coins of Aethelstan of about 930 bearing the name *Northwic*—the North town or trading centre—and the inference from coins in the Morley St Peter hoard that this mint was set up *c*. 920, show that it must have been a flourishing centre of commerce before this date and, from the primacy of its mint, the most important economic centre in East Anglia. But there is nothing to prove that Norwich before the Danish invasions of the late ninth century was more than a scattered riverine settlement on both sides of the Wensum, stretching from Barn Road in the west to the present Cathedral Close in the east. From this preDanish nucleus the village of Norwich developed in the late ninth and tenth centuries into an AngloDanish town which had spread chiefly southwards to occupy almost a square mile. Pottery, metalwork and churches indicate the extent of occupation and show that much of the area later enclosed by the Medieval walls was already inhabited by 1066. The position of this site at the confluence of the easily forded rivers Wensum and Yare and at the head of navigation, some 20 miles from the sea, was of vital importance in the growth of a town which served as a market for the surrounding countryside and as a port. Its large population is confirmed by the identification from dedications, documents and structural remains of about twentyfive churches which had been built by the late eleventh century. The importance of the Danish element is attested by such dedications as those of SS. Clement, Olave and Vedast, and by surviving street names of which Colegate, Cowgate, Finkelgate and Mountergate may be cited as examples. The name Pottergate and the discovery closeby of pottery wasters of Thetford ware indicate a Late Saxon pottery, and some clue to the town's commerce is provided by the import of pottery of St Neots' and Stamford wares from the East Midlands, though we are at present ignorant of its wider mercantile

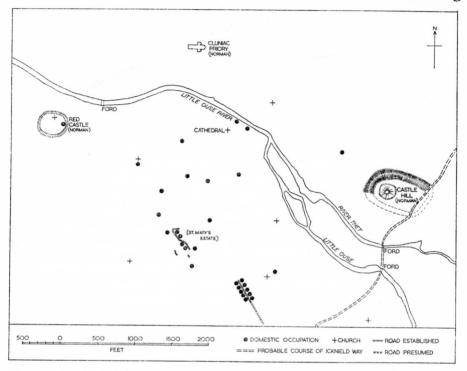

Fig. 40   Plan of Thetford, Norfolk, showing distribution of Saxo-Norman remains

activities. Clearly, however, the wealth of Norwich in Late Saxon times was intimately related both to the presence of Danes within the town and to the dense settlement of their kinsmen in the districts to the east and south, for whom it provided the obvious market.

At the Norman Conquest, Thetford was the second largest town in East Anglia, and a settlement on the site as early as 869 is clearly indicated by its selection as the winter quarters of the Danish army. The Anglo-Saxon Chronicle names it as *Theodford,* meaning the 'Chief Ford', and this probably refers to the adjacent fords over the rivers Little Ouse and Thet

Fig. 40

(now the Nun's Bridges) crossed by the Icknield Way. What little evidence we possess for the extent of Thetford before the arrival of the Danes in 869 suggests that it also was a small riverine settlement, perhaps founded in the sixth century on the south side of the Little Ouse inside and adjacent to the later Red Castle. This is close to another ford, called in recent centuries Ditchingford, which perhaps may have been an alternative crossing for the Icknield Way. It is just possible that the earlier name of this river crossing was *Redford*, under which name the town is mentioned in an Early Medieval chronicle, and that this Early Saxon settlement lost its separate identity in the late ninth-century expansion of a tiny village into a comparatively large town, henceforth all known as Thetford. Its establishment as a township resulted from the settlement of large numbers of Danes in 879 and the following years. This Anglo-Danish town stretched for almost a mile along the south side of the Little Ouse valley, from the site later occupied by Red Castle in the north-west to the traditional line of the Icknield Way in the south-east. It was defended on its western boundary by a rampart and ditch, some 40 feet across, which ran inland from the river for at least half a mile.

The excavations organized from 1948 onwards on a number of sites within the limits of the Anglo-Danish town have given us an unrivalled knowledge of its internal layout and develop-ment. From the late ninth century cobbled flint roadways were constructed, and these were repaired from time to time. The width of one was in places as much as 20 feet. A shallow double-ditch system associated with clay floors, huts and pits was detected, which was earlier than the earliest road and per-haps represents either the Danish winter quarters of 869 or the settlement of 879. During the tenth and early eleventh centuries these roads were flanked by scattered houses of various types. They were oval or rectangular buildings, occasionally two-storeyed, with walls of turfs or wattle set on sleeper beams, with thatched roofs, and floors usually sunk a foot or two into the natural sand. More than one hundred and eighty pits were found and most were filled with domestic refuse. Some had been storage pits, others were latrine pits, and two deep shafts were either wells or for tanning hides. No large buildings were discovered apart from a structure 50 feet long, which was divided into five rooms and has been interpreted as a boat-shaped house. The only masonry structures so far identified have been churches; at least twelve are recorded in the Domesday account of Thetford, but these constructions are unlikely to be earlier than the early eleventh century though they may, of course, replace churches of wattle-and-daub or timber.

Some of the inhabitants of Thetford were doubtless engaged in farming and thus helping to provide the food necessary for this large concentration of industrial and other workers. A ploughshare of this period has been found in Thetford, and remains of crops identified include oats and peas, the former perhaps being kiln-dried. Diet was diversified by the import of large quantities of shellfish (mussels, oysters, cockles and winkles) and by sea-fish, such as cod, whilst poachers apparently succeeded in hunting red and roe deer in the local woods as well as the more dangerous wild boar. Domestic life was en-livened by numerous cats and dogs, and at least one peacock may have graced an important feast.

At Domesday, Thetford was an administrative and com-mercial town comparable in size and status with Lincoln, Norwich and Oxford. A mint had been established c. 960–70, and men with Danish names like Grim and Brunstan are included among the moneyers. Despite the disasters of 1004 and 1010, when it went up in flames, Thetford was also an important industrial town. There is evidence of considerable working of iron and copper by metalsmiths, and the indications of weaving and spinning are so widespread as to suggest a domestic woollen industry based on the sheep grazing the Breckland heaths. This suggestion is confirmed by the concentration of sheep recorded in Breckland in the Domesday survey. The Anglo-Danes of Thetford were also deeply involved in the pottery industry. The Danes did not bring pottery with them, but as soon as they settled in Thetford in the late ninth century Rhenish potters established themselves in Thetford and probably in Ipswich and Norwich as well. Their output at Thetford was enormous, with thousands of cooking pots, flanged bowls and dishes, pitchers, storage-jars, crucibles and lamps being pro-duced in hard wheel-turned ware. Three kilns of the early eleventh century have been found and part of the last batch of pottery—cooking pots and lamps—was in one kiln when it was abandoned. This Thetford ware was traded over west Norfolk and into the Cambridge region, and even perhaps farther afield. But Thetford in its turn imported other wares, like the lead-glazed fabrics brought from Stamford as early as 900, and the shelly wares associated with St Neots and perhaps made in clamps in villages in the Huntingdon, Bedford and Cambridge areas. Trade between Thetford and the continent is shown by the import of lava millstones from the Rhineland, and by numerous small objects that are closely paralleled in the trading settlements of Holland and Schleswig-Holstein. So far, how-ever, none of the imported continental pottery of types dis-covered in ports such as London and *Hamwih* (Southampton) has been found at Thetford, though it would not be surprising if they came to light in Norwich or Ipswich.

Churches and monasteries were among the principal targets of the Danish onslaughts of 865 and 869, and most, if not all, were probably destroyed in those years. The episcopal organiza-tion certainly came to an end, for no bishops of Elmham were recorded for nearly a century after *c.* 870, and heathenism once again prevailed. It is to this period that the Danish place-name 'Ellough' in north-east Suffolk, indicating a heathen temple, is to be ascribed, and other pagan shrines were doubtless set up

Plate 51

in the principal areas of Danish settlement, for most of them remained pagan despite the nominal conversion of Guthrum. Christianity, however, probably survived among the Anglo⁄Saxon population of East Anglia with the permission of the Danish government, though the breakdown of the church organization, which led to a shortage of priests, must have seriously curtailed its activities. Little is known of the conversion of the East Anglian portion of the Danelaw, though the examples of Christian Wessex and Mercia were doubtless potent factors in the process. No attempt was made to recreate the former dioceses when East Anglia was reconquered by the English about 920, and the area was apparently placed under the charge of the Bishop of London until 956. In that year the Elmham diocese was re⁄established to include Suffolk as well as Norfolk, thus replacing the former dioceses of Dunwich and Elmham. It would appear probable that in the early tenth century a minster was built in each Hundred and manned by secular clergy who were responsible for the spiritual needs of its inhabitants. Although no minster buildings of the tenth century have been recognized in the area, they can be identified in the early eleventh century at Stoke⁄by⁄Clare and Sudbury, and large churches like Haddiscoe may prove to have been erected for this purpose. The sub⁄division of the areas served by the minsters into the smaller units known as parishes took place in the late tenth and early eleventh centuries, and it is during this period that the earliest of our surviving parish churches were erected by local landowners.

Some architectural details of these Late Saxon churches of the early eleventh century show once again the strong cultural influence of the Rhineland. The use of triangular⁄headed openings, windows set in the wall with a double splay, and windows with a mid⁄wall shaft between two narrow arches, are all technical features demonstrating foreign inspiration. The outstanding example of Late Saxon ecclesiastical construction

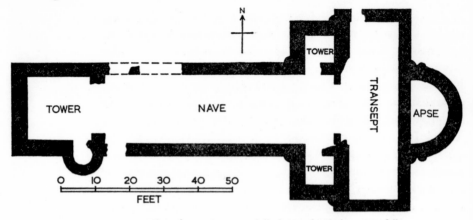

Fig. 41   Plan of Late Saxon cathedral. North Elmham, Norfolk

Plate 56

Fig. 41

in East Anglia, and, though small, one of the most important buildings of this period in all Britain, is the early eleventh-century cathedral at North Elmham, of which the ruins have been cleared and consolidated in recent years. The walls, almost entirely of local conglomerate, still stand about 10 feet high. In plan the building consists of an aisleless nave and a T-shaped transept with a shallow eastern apse, the whole having an internal length of 123 feet. The remains of a large tower survive at the west end, and there are also two small towers in the angles between the transept and nave. An even more remarkable structure was erected at Bury in 1021–32, when a circular tomb-chapel was provided for the translated body of St Edmund. Its form probably inspired the construction in the eleventh and following centuries of round towers for parish churches, a peculiarity of East Anglia that is represented by at least 160 examples. The scarcity of suitable local stone was an incentive, especially in Norfolk, for the construction in flint of round towers and windows, doorways and angles, fragments of stone being used only occasionally for some special function. In some churches this was supplemented by Roman bricks and tiles stripped from ruined buildings, and by the occasional manufacture of new bricks from the eleventh century onwards. In Suffolk, timber and clay-lump remained the most popular materials for church construction during the eleventh century, and stone was used even more sparingly than in Norfolk. A few coffin slabs of Barnack stone from Northamptonshire were brought to East Anglia in the late tenth and early eleventh centuries, and there decorated with interlaced ornament by masons strongly influenced by developments in Lincolnshire. Free-standing stone crosses in the same artistic style are rare in East Anglia, but fragments survive from two Norfolk churches, Whissonsett and Ringstead, as well as the mutilated cross-shaft of sandstone from the church of St Vedast, Norwich, which is decorated with interlace in the Scandinavian style. The vigorous treatment of figures of saints and beasts in this Anglo-Danish art style is well illustrated by the early eleventh-century stone carvings still decorating the church of St Nicholas at Ipswich. On the eve of the Norman Conquest, the cultural background of East Anglia reflected the fusion of the Rhenish, Scandinavian and native English traditions. Though temporarily submerged by Norman developments, Late Saxon traditions were to fuse with those of the conquerors and make their significant contribution to the greatest period of English ecclesiastical art.

Plate 55
Plate 54

CHAPTER X
Early Medieval East Anglia: an Epilogue

To do justice to Medieval East Anglia would require a volume in itself, but, even if space is lacking, it would be wrong to conclude our story at the Norman Conquest, for the Early Middle Ages form the culmination of the Late Saxon development. Some of the principal achievements of the period from 1066 to 1200 must therefore be noted.

The Anglo-Danish state was overthrown at Hastings and was gradually replaced by a centralized Norman régime, which soon impressed its might on its English subjects. Though few in numbers, the Norman aristocracy and its soldiery were able to suppress revolts by their military efficiency. This domination is witnessed archaeologically by numerous castles or private fortresses which were constructed at key points in the countryside. At least forty of these fortified bases, at first of earth and timber like Horsford Castle, and later of stone as at Castle Rising, were erected in East Anglia before 1200.

The religious zeal of the age was expressed by an impressive building development in the introduced Romanesque style, for numerous monasteries and parish churches were erected in the late eleventh and twelfth centuries. The remains of Castle Acre Priory give some idea of the scale of these new monasteries. By 1200 there were over eighty monasteries in Norfolk and Suffolk alone, and vast estates came under their control so that the Church became as important economically as it was spiritually. The Church made a significant contribution to the economic development of East Anglia in the Early Middle Ages, when the area of cultivated land was increased by the ploughing-up of heath and the felling of yet more woodland. Fresh villages

Plate 58
Plate 57

Plate 59

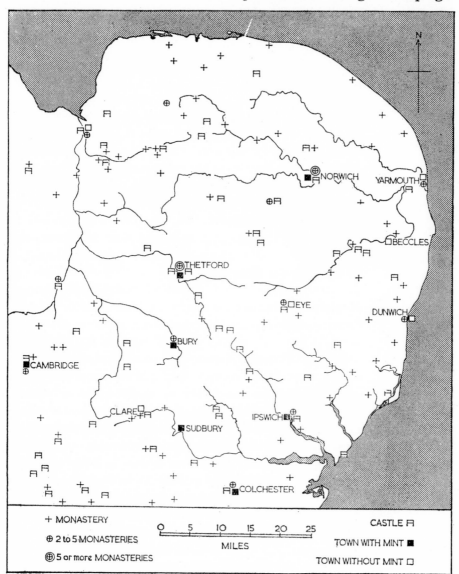

Fig. 42 Distribution of Early Medieval culture (1066–1200)

Fig. 42

Plate 60
Fig. 43

and hamlets were founded though on a smaller scale tha
Late Saxon times, and it is clear from many sources that
Anglia in the Early Medieval period was the most der
populated province in Britain. This concentration of industr
peasants, skilled artisans, merchants, soldiery and ecclesia
stimulated not only agriculture but other rural industries s
as salt⁄boiling, pottery⁄making and peat⁄cutting.

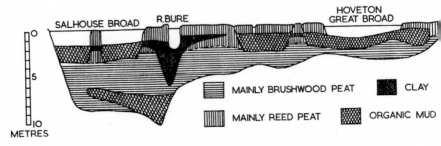

Fig. 43   Section of Medieval peat⁄pits. Salhouse and Hoveton Great Broads, Norfolk

Among the towns Norwich remained pre⁄eminent; by 1
it was probably the sixth largest town in England, ha
outstripped its old rival Thetford, for the wealth of Nort
grew with the agricultural development of eastern East An
Dunwich, Bury and Ipswich remained important centres
there were many smaller towns, some little more than vill
whose only claim to urban status lay in the temporary pos
sion of a mint or the right to hold a small market. The
Saxon trade with the Rhineland persisted throughout Med
times, but after the Conquest was supplemented by the prod
of Normandy—vast quantities of limestone for new edi
such as Norwich Cathedral and Castle, and pottery, prob
connected with the wine trade. The scale of East Anglian t
with the continent is well illustrated by the developmer

Lynn from a small settlement in the Late Saxon Age to the status by 1200 of the fifth largest port in England.

At the beginning of John's reign, then, East Anglia was one of the most prosperous provinces in Britain, with a dense and progressive population, whose achievements were to form the foundation of the area's industrial expansion in the Later Middle Ages and its agricultural revolution in the seventeenth and eighteenth centuries.

Important Visible Monuments in East Anglia

Only sites which are easily accessible and well-defined are included in this list, but those on private property are not necessarily open to the public without the permission of the owner or tenant. Sites in public ownership are indicated.

NEOLITHIC

ARMINGHALL 63/240061—Henge monument. Much ploughed but remains of bank visible.

DITCHINGHAM: Broome Heath 62/345914—long barrow.

RUDHAM, WEST: West Rudham Common 53/810253—long barrow.

WEETING: Grime's Graves 52/817898—flint mines. Two shafts open for inspection, many infilled shafts visible. Access by track from north. Ministry of Works.

BRONZE AGE

CRESSINGHAM, LITTLE 52/862988—group of round barrows, partly on heath, partly on arable; barrow containing celebrated Wessex culture burial now demolished.

NACTON 62/225412—group of round barrows in woodland. Near Orwell station.

SALTHOUSE: Salthouse Heath 63/075423—large group of round barrows extending into adjacent parishes of Cley and Kelling. Group ranges from Bell Beaker culture to Late Bronze Age.

IRON AGE

CLARE 52/768458—fort. Double ramparts and ditches, mutilated on south and east.

HOLKHAM 53/875447—fort on knoll in marsh, part of defences double. Approached by track leading north from Holkham church.

WARHAM 53/944409—fort. Double rampart and ditch, originally complete on west, enclosing 3½ acres. Approached by lane from east.

ROMAN

BURGH CASTLE 63/475046—coast defence fort (*Gariannonum*). Walls with bastions remain on three sides. Approached by lane from Burgh Castle church. Ministry of Works.

CAISTER-BY-YARMOUTH 63/517123—town. Remains of defences, 'hotel', street and Anglo-Saxon huts preserved after excavation. Ministry of Works.

CAISTOR-BY-NORWICH 63/230035—town. Defences. Street plan visible as crop-mark from opposite hill during drought conditions.

FRING, 5½ miles south-east of Hunstanton—Roman road (Peddar's Way) with well-preserved *agger*.

EARLY SAXON

BICHAMDICH—linear earthwork; best preserved portion 53/745083.

DEVIL'S DITCH—linear earthwork, just into Cambridgeshire but best example. North end 52/568660 and south end 52/653584.

FOSS DITCH—linear earthwork. North end 52/774959 and south end 52/756874.

LATE SAXON

ELMHAM, NORTH 53/988216—cathedral. Substantial remains incorporated in late fourteenth-century manor house. Ministry of Works.

EARLY MEDIEVAL

BINHAM 53/982399—Benedictine priory. Plan of monastic buildings preserved after clearing, nave of monastic church serves as parish church. Ministry of Works.

BURY ST EDMUNDS 52/857643—Benedictine abbey. Founded 1020; Norman gateway and west front of church survive, as well as extensive later Medieval buildings. Ministry of Works and Bury Corporation.

BURY ST EDMUNDS: Moyse's Hall, north end of Buttermarket— remains of late twelfth-century house utilized as museum. Bury Corporation.

CASTLE ACRE 53/815147—Cluniac priory. Extensive remains including fine west front of church. Ministry of Works.

CASTLE RISING 53/666246—stone keep and surrounding earthworks. Ministry of Works.

FRAMLINGHAM 62/286637—castle with late twelfth-century curtain wall, towers and ditch. Ministry of Works.

HAUGHLEY 62/024626—Norman motte-and-bailey castle, with wet moat.

HORSFORD 63/205157—Norman motte-and-bailey castle with scanty remains of later stone keep.

ORFORD 62/419499—late twelfth-century polygonal stone keep on earlier motte. Ministry of Works.

THETFORD: Castle Hill 52/875828—Norman motte-and-bailey castle. Motte highest in Britain; earthworks of bailey probably incorporate ramparts of Iron Age camp. Thetford Corporation.

THETFORD 52/865835—Cluniac priory. Extensive remains of Norman and later buildings. Ministry of Works.

Museums

Containing important collections of East Anglian archaeological material

BURY ST EDMUNDS, Moyse's Hall.

CAMBRIDGE, University Museum of Archaeology and Ethnology.

COLCHESTER, Colchester and Essex Museum.

IPSWICH, Museum of Natural History, Archaeology and Ethnology.

KING'S LYNN, Museum and Art Gallery.

LONDON, British Museum, Depts. of British and Medieval Antiquities, and Coins and Medals.

MILDENHALL, Museum of Mildenhall Natural History and Archaeological Society.

NORWICH, Castle Museum.

OXFORD, Ashmolean Museum.

SANDRINGHAM, Estate Museum.

THETFORD, Ancient House Museum.

Bibliography

GENERAL WORKS

COPLEY, G. J., *An Archaeology of S.E. England—A study in continuity,* London, 1958.

FOX, SIR C., *The Archaeology of the Cambridge Region* (with supplement), Cambridge, 1948.

FOX, SIR C., 'The Distribution of Man in East Anglia, *c.* 2300 B.C.– A.D. 50', *Proc. Prehist. Soc. E. Anglia,* VII, 1933, pp. 149–64.

SAINTY, J. E., AND CLARKE, R. R., 'A Century of Norfolk Prehistory', *Norf. Arch.,* XXIX, 1946, pp. 8–40.

Norfolk Archaeology.

Proceedings of the Suffolk Institute of Archaeology.

Communications, or Proceedings, of the Cambridge Antiquarian Society.

Victoria County History. Norfolk, Suffolk and *Cambridgeshire.* Articles on Early Man, Romano-British and Anglo-Saxon Remains, and Medieval History and Archaeology.

CHAPTER I

GODWIN, H., *The History of the British Flora,* Cambridge, 1956.

GODWIN, H., AND CLIFFORD, M. H., 'Studies in the Post-glacial History of British Vegetation', *Phil. Trans. Roy. Soc. Lond.,* Ser. B, CCXXIX, 1938, pp. 323–406 and CCXXX, 1940, pp. 239–303.

GODWIN, H., AND TALLANTIRE, P. A., 'Hockham Mere, Norfolk', *Journ. Ecology,* XXXIX, 1951, pp. 285–307.

LAMBERT, J. M., ETC. 'The Making of the Broads', *Roy. Geographical Soc. Memoir,* London, 1960.

MOSBY, J. E. G., *The Land of Britain: Part 70—Norfolk,* London, 1938.

ROXBY, P. M., 'East Anglia', in *Essays in Regional Geography* (ed. Ogilvie), London, 1928.

CHAPTER II

LANKESTER, SIR E. R., 'Description of the Test Specimen of the Rostro-carinate Industry found beneath the Norwich Crag', *Roy. Anthrop. Inst. Occ. Paper No. 4,* 1914.

MOIR, J. R., 'Further discoveries of Humanly Fashioned Flints in and beneath the Red Crag of Suffolk', *Proc. Prehist. Soc. E. Anglia*, III, 1921, pp. 389–430.

MOIR, J. R., AND HOPWOOD, A. T., 'Excavations at Brundon, Suffolk', (1935–7), *Proc. Prehist. Soc.*, V, 1939, pp. 1–32.

OAKLEY, K., 'Tools Makyth Man', *Antiq.*, XXXI, 1957, pp. 199–209.

PATERSON, T. T., AND FAGG, B. E. B., 'Studies in the Palaeolithic Succession in England: No. 1, The Barnham Sequence', *Proc. Prehist. Soc.*, III, 1937, pp. 87–135; 'No. 2, The Upper Brecklandian Acheul (Elveden)', *Proc. Prehist. Soc.*, VI, 1940, pp. 1–29.

SAINTY, J. E., 'An Acheulean Palaeolithic Workshop Site at Whitlingham, near Norwich', *Proc. Prehist. Soc. E. Anglia*, V, 1927, pp. 177–213.

WARREN, S. H., 'The Crag Platform—its Geology and Archaeological Problems', *S. E. Nat. & Antiq.*, LIII, 1948, pp. 48–52.

WEST, R. G., 'The Quaternary Deposits of Hoxne, Suffolk', *Phil. Trans. Roy. Soc. Lond.*, Ser. B, CCXXXIX, 1956, pp. 265–356.

WEST, R. G., 'The Pleistocene Epoch in East Anglia', *Journ. Glaciology*, III, 1958, pp. 211–16.

WEST, R. G., AND McBURNEY, C. M. B., 'The Quaternary Deposits at Hoxne, Suffolk, and their Archaeology', *Proc. Prehist. Soc.*, XX, 1954, pp. 131–54.

ZEUNER, F. E., *Dating the Past*, 4th ed., London, 1958.

CHAPTER III

CLARK, J. G. D., *The Mesolithic Age in Britain*, Cambridge, 1932.

CLARK, J. G. D., 'A Microlithic Industry from the Cambridgeshire Fenland and other Industries of Sauveterrian affinities from Britain', *Proc. Prehist. Soc.*, XXI, 1955, pp. 3–20.

CLARK, J. G. D., GODWIN, H., AND M. E., ETC., 'Report on recent excavations at Peacock's Farm, Shippea Hill, Cambridgeshire', *Ant. Journ.*, XV, 1935, pp. 284–319. (Also for Chapter IV.)

SAINTY, J. E., 'Mesolithic Sites in Norfolk', *Norf. Arch.*, XXVIII, 1945, pp. 234–7.

BRISCOE, G., 'Combined Beaker and Iron Age sites at Lakenheath, Suffolk', *Proc. Camb. Ant. Soc.,* XLII, 1949, pp. 92–111. (Also for Chapter VI.)

BRISCOE, G., 'A Windmill Hill site at Hurst Fen, Mildenhall', *Proc. Camb. Ant. Soc.,* XLVII, 1954, pp. 13–24.

BRISCOE, G., 'Swale's Tumulus: a Combined Neolithic "A" and Bronze Age Barrow at Worlington, Suffolk', *Proc. Camb. Ant. Soc.,* L, 1957, pp. 101–12.

CLARK, J. G. D., 'The Timber Monument at Arminghall and its Affinities', *Proc. Prehist. Soc.,* II, 1936, pp. 1–51.

CLARK, J. G. D., GODWIN, H., AND M. E., ETC., 'Report on an Early Bronze Age site in the S. E. Fens', *Ant. Journ.,* XIII, 1933, pp. 266–96.

CLARKE, W. G. (ed), 'Report on the Excavations at Grime's Graves, Weeting, 1914', *Prehist. Soc. E. Anglia Rep.,* 1915.

GLENDENNING, S. E., 'A Handled Beaker from Bodney, Norfolk', *Proc. Prehist. Soc. E. Anglia,* VII, 1932, pp. 107–10.

HOGG, A. H. A., 'A Long Barrow at West Rudham, Norfolk', *Norf. Arch.,* XXVII, 1940, pp. 315–31.

PIGGOTT, S., *The Neolithic Cultures of the British Isles,* Cambridge, 1954.

PIGGOTT, S., 'Windmill Hill—East or West?' *Proc. Prehist. Soc.,* XXI, 1955, pp. 96–101.

SMITH, I. F., 'Late Beaker Pottery from Lyonesse Surface and the date of the Transgression', *Univ. Lond. Inst. Arch., 11th Ann. Report,* 1955, pp. 29–42.

WARREN, S. H., PIGGOTT, S., ETC., 'The Archaeology of the Submerged Land-surface of the Essex Coast', *Proc. Prehist. Soc.,* II, 1936, pp. 178–210.

WARREN, S. H., AND SMITH, I. F., 'Neolithic Pottery from the Submerged Land-surface of the Essex Coast', *Univ. Lond. Inst. Arch., 10th Ann. Report,* 1954, pp. 26–33.

CHAPTER V

CAWDOR, EARL, AND FOX, C., 'The Beacon Hill Barrow, Barton Mills, Suffolk', *Proc. Camb. Ant. Soc.,* XXVI, 1925, pp. 19–65.

CLARK, J. G. D., 'Report on a Late Bronze Age site in Mildenhall Fen, West Suffolk', *Ant. Journ.,* XVI, 1936, pp. 29–50.

CLARKE, R. R., 'Gold Ornaments of the Bronze Age from Norfolk', *Arch. Journ.* CVI, 1951, pp. 57–8.

GRINSELL, L. V., *The Ancient Burial-Mounds of England*, 2nd. ed., London, 1953.

Inventaria Archaeologia. Great Britain (Bronze Hoards), London, 1955.

JONES, H., 'On the Discovery . . . of a Pile Dwelling in Barton Mere near Bury St Edmunds', Q. *J. Suff. Inst.,* 1869, pp. 31–6.

LETHBRIDGE, T. C., 'Excavation of the Snailwell Group of Bronze Age Barrows', *Proc. Camb. Ant. Soc.,* XLIII, 1950, pp. 30–49.

PIGGOTT, S., 'The Early Bronze Age in Wessex', *Proc. Prehist. Soc.,* IV, 1938, pp. 52–106.

CHAPTER VI

ALLEN, D., 'The Belgic Dynasties of Britain and Their Coins', *Archaeologia,* XC, 1944, pp. 1–46.

BRISCOE, G., 'Combined Early Iron Age and Romano-British site at Wangford, West Suffolk', *Proc. Camb. Ant. Soc.,* LI, 1958, pp. 19–29. (Also Chapter VII.)

CLARK, J. G. D., AND FELL, C. I., 'The Early Iron Age Site at Micklemoor Hill, West Harling, Norfolk, and its Pottery', *Proc. Prehist. Soc.,* XIX, 1953, pp. 1–40.

CLARKE, R. R., 'The Iron Age in Norfolk and Suffolk', *Arch. Journ.,* XCVI, 1940, pp. 1–113 and 223–5.

CLARKE, R. R., 'A Hoard of Metalwork of the Early Iron Age from Ringstead, Norfolk', *Proc. Prehist. Soc.,* XVII, 1952, pp. 214–25.

CLARKE, R. R., 'The Early Iron Age Treasure from Snettisham, Norfolk', *Proc. Prehist. Soc.,* XX, 1954, pp. 27–86.

CLARKE, R. R., 'A Hoard of Silver Coins of the Iceni from Honingham, Norfolk', *Brit. Num. Journ.,* XXVIII, 1956, pp. 1–10.

CLARKE, R. R., AND HAWKES, C. F. C., 'An Iron Anthropoid Sword from Shouldham, Norfolk, with Related Continental and British Weapons', *Proc. Prehist. Soc.,* XXI, 1955, pp. 198–227.

FOX, SIR C., *Pattern and Purpose—a Survey of Early Celtic Art in Britain,* Cardiff, 1958.

GRAY, H. St. G., 'Trial Excavations . . . at Warham, near Wells, Norfolk', *Ant. Journ.,* XIII, 1933, pp. 399–413.

HARTLEY, B. R., 'The Wandlebury Iron Age Hill-Fort, Excavations of 1955–6', *Proc. Camb. Ant. Soc.,* L, 1957, pp. 1–27.

HAWKES, C. F. C., 'An Early Settlement at Runcton Holme—The Second Occupation—A Peasant Settlement of the Iceni', *Proc. Prehist. Soc. E. Anglia,* VII, 1933, pp. 231–62.

HAWKES, C. F. C., AND HULL, M. R., *Camulodunum,* London, 1947.

LETHBRIDGE, T. C., 'Burial of an Iron Age Warrior at Snailwell', *Proc. Camb. Ant. Soc.,* XLVII, 1954, pp. 25–37.

RADFORD, C. A. R., 'The Tribes of Southern Britain', *Proc. Prehist. Soc.,* XX, 1954, pp. 1–26.

CHAPTER VII

ATKINSON, D., 'The Roman Villa of Gayton Thorpe', *Norf. Arch.,* XXIII, 1928, pp. 166–209.

ATKINSON, D., 'Caistor Excavations, 1929', *Norf Arch.,* XXIV, 1931, pp. 93–139.

ATKINSON, D., 'Roman Pottery from Caistor-next-Norwich', *Norf. Arch.,* XXVI, 1937, pp. 197–230.

BRAILSFORD, J. W., *The Mildenhall Treasure—a Handbook,* Brit. Mus., 1955.

BRISCOE, G., 'A Romano-British Settlement at Lakenheath, Suffolk', *Proc. Suff. Inst. Arch.,* XXVI, 1953, pp. 71–84.

CLARK, J. G. D., 'Report on Excavations on the Cambridgeshire Car Dyke, 1947', *Ant. Journ.,* XXIX, 1949, pp. 145–63.

CLARKE, R. R., 'The Roman Villages at Brettenham and Needham and the Contemporary Road System', *Norf. Arch.,* XXVI, 1937, pp. 123–63.

CLARKE, R. R., 'Roman Norfolk since Haverfield—a Survey of Discovery from 1901', *Norf. Arch.,* XXX, 1950, pp. 140–55.

FRERE, S. S., 'A Claudian Site at Needham, Norfolk', *Ant. Journ.,* XXI, 1941, pp. 40–55.

GREEN, C. (Interim reports on excavations at Caister-by-Yarmouth), *Journ. Roman Studies,* XLII–XLV, 1952–5.

HAWKES, C. F. C., 'Caistor-by-Norwich: the Roman Town of *Venta Icenorum*', *Arch. Journ.,* CVI, 1951, pp. 62–5.

MARGARY, I. D., *Roman Roads in Britain,* I, London, 1955, pp. 212–46.

MAYNARD, G., BROWN, B., ETC., 'Reports on a Roman pottery-making site at Foxledge Common, Wattisfield, Suffolk', *Proc. Suff. Inst. Arch.*, XXII, 1936, pp. 178–97.

MOIR, J. R., AND MAYNARD, G., 'The Roman Villa at Castle Hill, Whitton, Ipswich', *Proc. Suff. Inst. Arch.*, XXI, 1933, pp. 240–62.

MOORE, I. E., 'Roman Suffolk', *Proc. Suff. Inst. Arch.*, XXIV, 1949, pp. 163–81.

MORRIS, A. J., 'The Saxon Shore Fort at Burgh Castle', *Proc. Suff. Inst. Arch.*, XXIV, 1949, pp. 100–20. (Also for Chapter VIII.)

MYRES, J. N. L., 'Romano-Saxon Pottery', in *Dark-Age Britain* (ed. Harden), London, 1956, pp. 16–39.

ORDNANCE SURVEY, Map of Roman Britain, 3rd. ed., Chessington, 1956.

PHILLIPS, C. W., 'The Fenland Research Committee: its past achieve-ments and future prospects', in *Aspects of Archaeology* (ed. Grimes), London, 1951, pp. 258–73.

RIVET, A. L. F., *Town and Country in Roman Britain,* London, 1958.

ST. JOSEPH, J. K. S., 'The Roman Fort at Brancaster', *Ant. Journ.,* XVI, 1936, pp. 444–60.

TOYNBEE, J. M. C., AND CLARKE, R. R., 'A Roman Decorated Helmet and other Objects from Norfolk', *Journ. Roman Studies,* XXXVIII, 1948, pp. 20–7.

CHAPTER VIII

BRUCE-MITFORD, R. L. S., *The Sutton Hoo Ship-Burial: a provisional guide,* Brit. Mus., 1947.

BRUCE-MITFORD, R. L. S., 'Saxon Rendlesham', *Proc. Suff. Inst. Arch.,* XXIV, 1949, pp. 228–51.

BRUCE-MITFORD, R. L. S., 'The Sutton Hoo Ship-Burial: Recent Theories and some comments on general interpretation', *Proc. Suff. Inst. Arch.,* XXV, 1950, pp. 1–78.

BRUCE-MITFORD, R. L. S., 'The Snape Boat-grave', *Proc. Suff. Inst. Arch.,* XXVI, 1952, pp. 1–26.

CLARKE, R. R. (AND MYRES, J. N. L.), 'Norfolk in the Dark Ages, A.D. 400–800', *Norf. Arch.,* XXVII, 1939–40, pp. 163–249.

CLARKE, R. R., 'An Ogham inscribed Knife-handle from S. W. Norfolk', *Ant. Journ.,* XXXII, 1952, pp. 71–3.

CLARKE, R. R., 'The Foss Ditch—a Linear Earthwork in S. W. Norfolk', *Norf. Arch.*, XXXI, 1955, pp. 178–96. (Also for Chapter VII.)

FOX, C., 'Dykes', *Antiq.*, III, 1929, pp. 135–54.

HODGKIN, R. H., *A History of the Anglo-Saxons*, 3rd ed., Oxford, 1952.

HURST, J. G., AND WEST, S. E., 'An Account of Middle Saxon Ipswich Ware', *Proc. Camb. Ant. Soc.*, L, 1957, pp. 29–42.

LAYARD, N. F., 'An Anglo-Saxon Cemetery in Ipswich', *Archaeologia*, LX, 1907, pp. 325–52.

LEEDS, E. T., 'Denmark and Early England', *Ant. Journ.*, XXVI, 1946, pp. 22–37.

LETHBRIDGE, T. C., *Recent Excavations in Anglo-Saxon Cemeteries in Cambridgeshire and Suffolk*, Cambridge, 1931.

LETHBRIDGE, T. C., *A Cemetery at Lackford, Suffolk*, Cambridge, 1951.

LETHBRIDGE, T. C., 'The Anglo-Saxon Settlement in Eastern England —a reassessment', in *Dark Age Britain* (ed. Harden), London, 1956, pp. 112–22.

CHAPTER IX

CLAPHAM, A. W., AND GODFREY, W. H., 'The Saxon Cathedral of Elmham', *Ant. Journ.*, VI, 1926, pp. 402–9.

CLARKE, R. R., AND DOLLEY, R. H. M., 'The Morley St Peter Hoard', *Antiq.*, XXXII, 1958, pp. 100–3.

DARBY, H. C., *The Domesday Geography of Eastern England*, Cambridge, 1952. (Also for Chapters I and X.)

DAVIS, R. H. C., 'East Anglia and the Danelaw', *Trans. Roy. Hist. Soc.*, V, Ser. 5, 1955, pp. 23–39.

DUNNING, G. C., 'The Saxon Town of Thetford', *Arch. Journ.*, CVI, 1951, pp. 72–3.

EKWALL, E., 'The Scandinavian Settlement', in *An Historical Geography of England before A.D. 1800* (ed. Darby), 1936, pp. 133–64.

EKWALL, E., *The Concise Oxford Dictionary of English Place-Names*, 3rd ed., Oxford, 1947.

HERVEY, LORD FRANCIS, *Corolla Sancti Eadmundi*, London, 1907.

HURST, J. G., 'Saxo-Norman Pottery in East Anglia', *Proc. Camb. Ant. Soc.*, XLIX, 1956, pp. 43–70; L, 1957, pp. 29–60; LI, 1958, pp. 37–65.

JOPE, E. M., 'Excavations in the City of Norwich, 1948', *Norf. Arch.,* XXX, 1952, pp. 287–323.

KNOCKER, G. M., AND HUGHES, R. G., 'Thetford Excavations', *Arch. News Letter,* II, 1950, pp. 117–22.

CHAPTER X

ALLISON, K. J., 'The Lost Villages of Norfolk', *Norf. Arch.,* XXXI, 1955, pp. 116–62.

CAUTLEY, H. M., *Suffolk Churches and Their Treasures,* London, 1937.

CAUTLEY, H. M., *Norfolk Churches,* Ipswich, 1949.

DARBY, H. C., *The Medieval Fenland,* Cambridge, 1940.

DOUGLAS, D. C., *The Social Structure of Medieval East Anglia,* Oxford, 1927.

HURST, J. G., AND GOLSON, J., 'Excavations at St Benedict's Gates, Norwich, 1951 and 1953', *Norf. Arch.,* XXXI, 1955, pp. 1–112.

KNOWLES, D., AND HADCOCK, R. N., *Medieval Religious Houses, England and Wales,* London, 1953.

Sources of Illustrations

The photographs for the plates are from the Norwich Castle Museum collection (taken by Hallam Ashley, F.R.P.S.) except for the following: British Museum (25, 28, 34, 36, 37, 41, 42, 45–9, 53); Museum of Archaeology and Ethnology, Cambridge (3); Ipswich Museum (38); University of Cambridge (Photo by J. K. St. Joseph, Crown Copyright Reserved) (6, 29, 30, 31, 59, 60); Royal Air Force, Crown Copyright Reserved (12, 27); Aerofilms Ltd (57); Norfolk and Norwich Aero Club (58); Ministry of Works (33, 50, 51); Bury Free Press (18); Norfolk News Co. (44); Thames & Hudson (10, 26); Executors of the late A. L. Armstrong (9); and H. Ashley, F.R.P.S. (1, 2, 7, 32, 55). Permission to reproduce these photographs is acknowledged with gratitude.

The maps and most of the plans are from the author's originals re-drawn by his assistant, D. R. Howlett, who has also produced original drawings of objects in Norwich Castle Museum (figs. 14, 19, 34, 38) and Ipswich Museum (fig. 23) and has adapted plans or drawings by J. E. Turner (fig. 22), J. G. D. Clark (fig. 24), C. Green and Ministry of Works (fig. 30), Ipswich Museum (figs. 31, 33), J. G. Hurst and S. E. West (fig. 35), A. W. Clapham and W. H. Godfrey (fig. 41), R. R. Clarke and G. M. Knocker (fig. 40) and Miss J. M. Lambert (fig. 43), to all of whom grateful acknowledgement is made. Fig. 25 is based on an original sketch by J. E. Turner. Miss S. C. Puddy of the Norwich Museums' staff has made original drawings of objects in that museum (figs. 3, 4, 7, 8, 11, 12, 16); in the Museum of Archaeology and Ethnology, Cambridge (fig. 27), and in the British Museum (figs. 18, 28). She has re-drawn illustrations by J. R. Moir (fig. 5), J. G. D. Clark (fig. 9) and a drawing in the possession of the Society of Antiquaries of London (fig. 36). The co-operation of these individuals and organizations is hereby acknowledged.

3

4

5

6

7

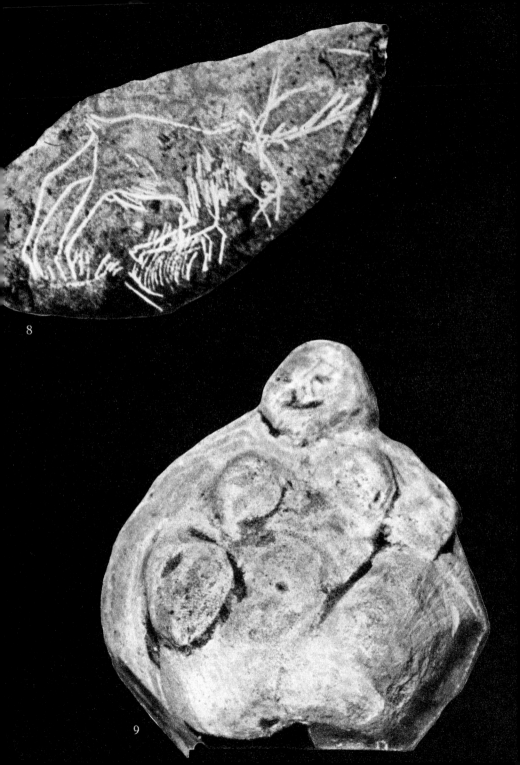

8

9

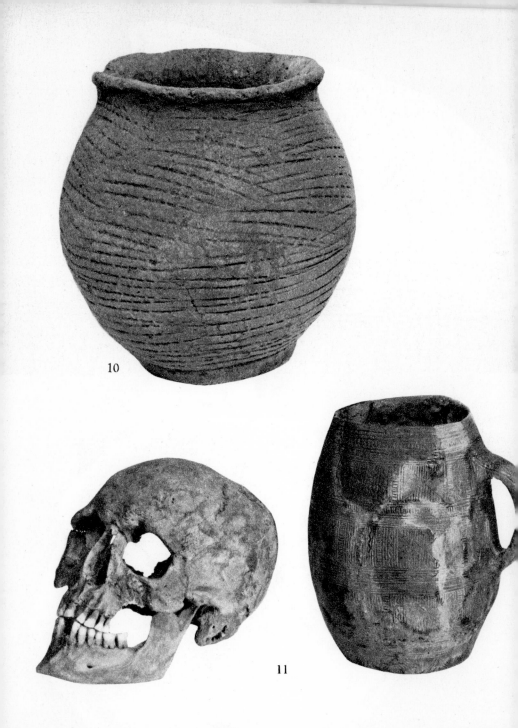

10

11

13

14

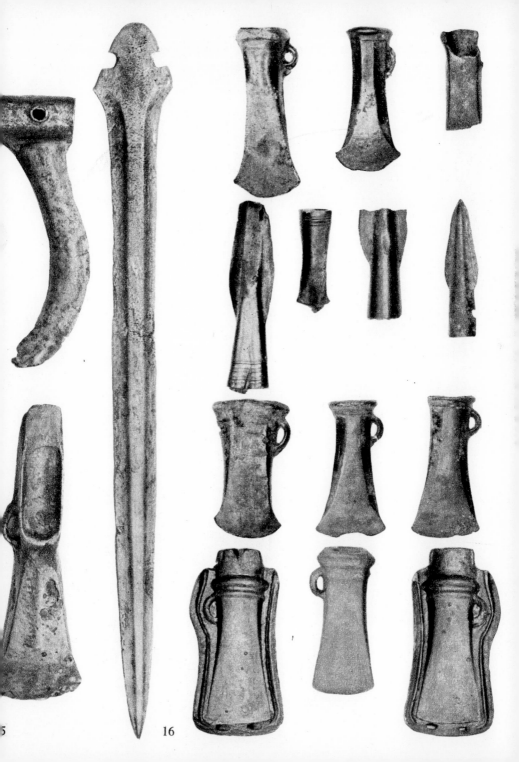

15   16

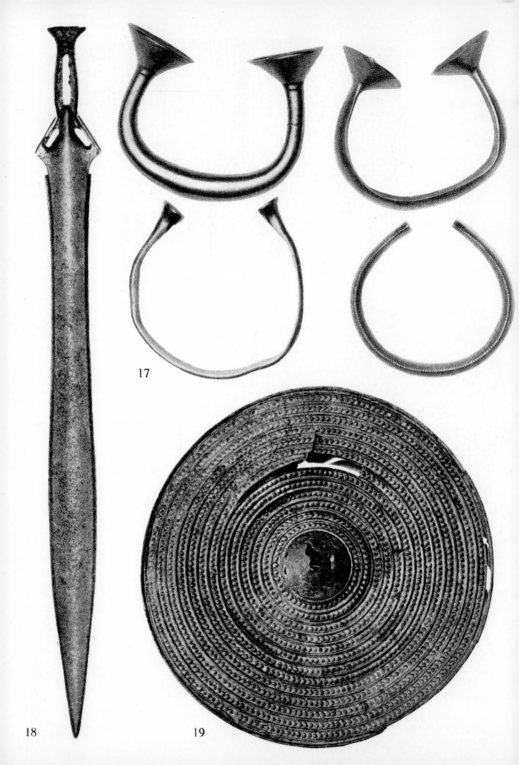

17

18 19

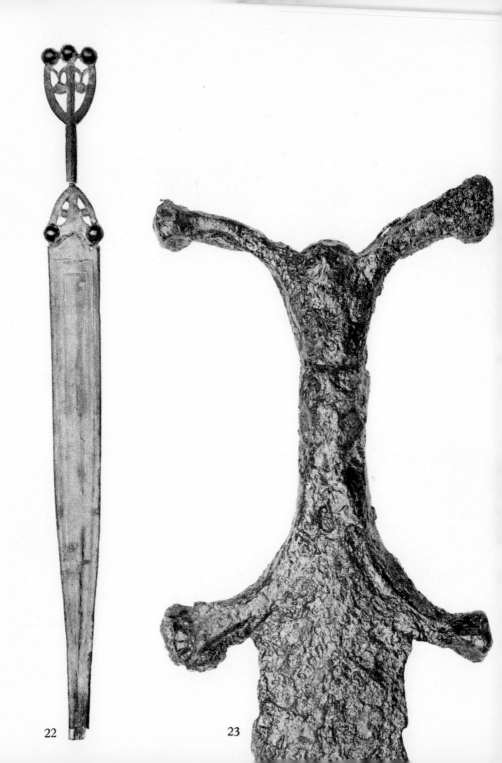

22   23

26

27

29

30

32

33

34

35

36

37

8

39

40

41

42

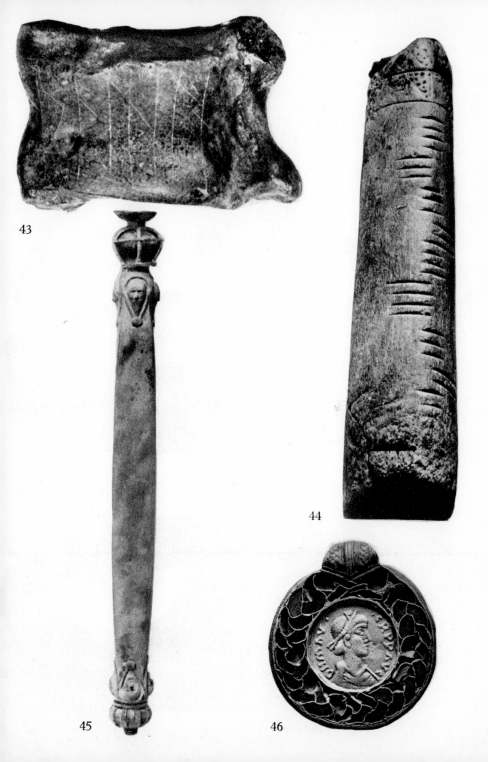

43

44

45 46

47

48

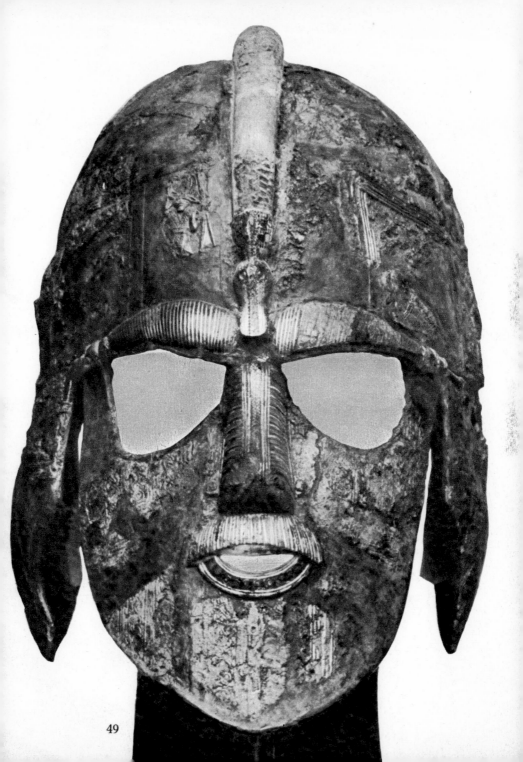

49

51

52

53

54

55

56

57

58

59

Notes on the Plates

1 Typical Breckland scenery at Bodney, Norfolk. This region was one of the principal centres of population during most of the periods covered by this book. The modern road forms part of the course of the prehistoric Icknield Way.

2 View of the valley of the River Blyth in the Sandlings region. This region was once the main centre of population in East Suffolk.

3 Pottery bowl of Phase II of the Windmill Hill culture, from Mildenhall, Suffolk. Height $7\frac{1}{4}$ in. Museum of Archaeology and Ethnology, Cambridge.

4 Barbed point of red deer antler forming prong of Mesolithic fish-spear. It was trawled from the Leman and Ower Banks some 25 miles north-east of Cromer. Length $8\frac{3}{4}$ in. Norwich Castle Museum.

5 Lower stone of sandstone saddle-quern from Middleton, Norfolk. Corn-grinding stones of this type were in common use from the Neolithic until towards the end of the Iron Age. Length $17\frac{1}{4}$ in. Norwich Castle Museum.

6 Air view of the infilled shafts of the Neolithic flint mines of Grime's Graves at Weeting, Norfolk.

7 Mine gallery at Grime's Graves. The dark layer in the chalk is composed of nodules of the best quality flint—the 'floorstone'.

8 Red deer incised on flint crust from Grime's Graves. Drawings of this type, perhaps for magical purposes, show Mesolithic influence and can be compared with Scandinavian developments of Neolithic date. Length $3\frac{1}{4}$ in. British Museum.

9 Chalk figurine of a pregnant woman from Grime's Graves. This figure probably represents the Earth Goddess, and formed part of a ritual assemblage at the base of Pit 15. Height $4\frac{1}{4}$ in. British Museum.

10   Pottery bell beaker from Bawdsey, Suffolk. This type of vessel was introduced in the Late Neolithic and continued in use into the Early Bronze Age. Height 4¼ in. Ipswich Museum.

11   Handled pottery beaker and associated human skull of Early Bronze Age date from a burial at Bodney, Norfolk. Height of beaker 8 in. Norwich Castle Museum.

12   The vertical air-photograph which led to the discovery of the henge-monument at Arminghall, Norfolk. The dark inner circle represents the inner ditch surrounding the central sanctuary in which the post-holes are visible as black dots. The thin outer ring corresponds with the outer ditch.

13   Pottery food-vessel from Needham, Norfolk. This vessel contained a cremation of Early Bronze Age date. Height 5⅝ in. Norwich Castle Museum.

14   Wessex culture grave-goods found with a male inhumation under a round barrow at Little Cressingham, Norfolk, in 1849. These comprise a grooved bronze dagger, which formerly had a wooden hilt (length of surviving fragment 8 in.); a flat bronze dagger; a necklace of amber beads and pendants; a thin, rectangular gold plate (length 3½ in.), and other sheet gold mountings. Norwich Castle Museum.

15   Middle Bronze Age bronze hoard from Downham Market, Norfolk, consisting of a rapier blade (length 15 in.), a socketed sickle and a looped palstave. Museum of Archaeology and Ethnology, Cambridge.

16   Late Bronze Age bronze hoard from Unthank Road, Norwich. This hoard consists of six socketed axeheads, four spearheads and the two halves of a bronze mould for casting socketed axeheads, besides other fragments not shown in the photograph. The axehead between the halves of the mould is a tinted plaster cast taken from it. Length of mould 5½ in. Norwich Castle Museum.

17 Late Bronze Age gold hoard from Caister-by-Yarmouth, Norfolk. The two upper ornaments are a well-known Irish type, and are usually termed cloak-fasteners. The other two objects are bracelets. Maximum diameter of larger cloak-fastener 3 in. Norwich Castle Museum.

18 Late Bronze Age bronze sword from Lawshall, Suffolk. This is an example of the straight-shouldered type of slashing sword made between 800 and 600 B.C. Length 23½ in. Bury Museum.

19 Late Bronze Age bronze shield from Sutton, Norfolk, decorated with concentric circles of small bosses and raised rings. Diameter 20½ in. Norwich Castle Museum.

20 Iron Age A pottery bowl from Cromer, Norfolk. This burnished and decorated bowl represents one of the types of finely textured pot made by the Iron Age A invaders and their successors. The base is decorated with incised triangular patterns. Height 5½in. Norwich Castle Museum.

21 Late Bronze Age cinerary urn from Salthouse, Norfolk. This undecorated biconical urn, which contained cremated bones, was discovered in a round barrow of the Salthouse Heath group. Height 17 in. Norwich Castle Museum.

22 Iron Age pseudo-anthropoid dagger from 'Hertford Warren', an unidentified locality believed to be near Bury St Edmunds, Suffolk. This bronze-hilted iron dagger, derived from the anthropoid type, is probably a Marnian import of the second century B.C. Original length at least 14 in. Saffron Walden Museum.

23 Hilt of anthropoid sword of Iron Age date from Shouldham, Norfolk. This iron sword was found lying across the chest of a skeleton of a Marnian warrior, probably of the late third century B.C. The pommel knob depicts a 'gloomy' human face. Length of hilt 3¼ in., length of sword 21⅜ in. Norwich Castle Museum.

24 Detail of decoration of a side-link of a bridle-bit from the hoard found
at Ringstead, Norfolk. This bit forms one of a pair, doubtless for the
two ponies of a chariot of the first century B.C. This decoration is a
fine example of the skill of a metalworker of eastern England. Over-all
length of bit $10\frac{1}{4}$ in., diameter of knob $\frac{9}{10}$ in. Norwich Castle Museum.

25 Ring terminal torc of gold alloy from Hoard E of the Iron Age treasure
from Snettisham, Norfolk. This elaborately ornamented necklet was
probably made in eastern England during the late first century B.C.
A quarter-stater of the Gaulish Atrebates was found inside one terminal.
Diameter of hoop 8 in. British Museum. Replica in Norwich Castle
Museum.

26 Pottery butt-beaker of Belgic type from an early first century A.D.
cremation cemetery at Boxford, Suffolk. Height 9 in. Ipswich Museum.

27 Vertical air view of Iron Age fort, Warham Camp, Warham St Mary,
Norfolk. Excavations in 1914 and 1959 suggest that it was constructed
in the late first century B.C. or early first century A.D. The circuit of the
inner and outer ramparts was once complete, and encloses an area of
$3\frac{1}{2}$ acres. In the field immediately north-east the unfinished ditch of a
rectangular fort of similar date was partially excavated in 1959.

28 Roman bronze head of the Emperor Claudius from the River Alde,
Rendham, Suffolk. This head, probably of Gaulish workmanship, had
been hacked from a statue which may have stood in a public building at
Camulodunum destroyed in the Boudiccan revolt A.D. 60–1. Height
12 in. Collection: Mrs E. R. Hollond.

29 Air view of Roman signal station at Thornham, Norfolk, looking east.
The south-east corner was destroyed when digging a pit, now overgrown
with trees. Excavation in 1952, 1955 and 1956 suggests that this enclosure
was constructed soon after the Boudiccan revolt of A.D. 60–1, probably
in connection with a ferry-service across the Wash from the Lincolnshire
coast. Within the enclosure of about $\frac{1}{2}$ acre was discovered a small inhumation cemetery of sixth/seventh century A.D. Grave-goods were
associated with some of the bodies.

30 Air view of Roman walled town at Caistor-by-Norwich, Norfolk, looking east. This shows the central part of the town with its grid-iron street pattern, surrounded by a wall (represented by hedge lines) erected *c*. A.D. 200. The Medieval parish church is visible near the south-east corner.

31 Air view of Roman field-system in Fenland, Downham West, Norfolk. The Roman fields can be seen as dark rectangles running obliquely to the modern field boundaries beyond the Old Bedford River. A considerable amount of Roman pottery has come from this site.

32 South-east corner bastion of Roman coast-defence fort, Burgh Castle, Suffolk. Only the upper part of the bastion is bonded to the fort wall, thus indicating that the plan was modified during construction. A socket in the top of the bastion was for a spring gun.

33 Air view of Roman coast-defence fortress, Burgh Castle, Suffolk. The flint and brick walls (the west wall nearest the River Waveney has been removed) enclose about 6 acres and were erected in the late third century. Excavation in 1958 revealed traces of the seventh-century monastery of St Fursey. Later the enclosure served as a bailey for a Norman motte-and-bailey castle.

34 Roman cavalry helmet of gilding metal dredged from River Wensum at Worthing, Norfolk. This ceremonial helmet is decorated with sea-dragons, an eagle's head and feathers, and snakes. Height $9\frac{1}{2}$ in. Norwich Castle Museum.

35 Visor-mask of Roman cavalry helmet of gilding metal from the River Wensum at Worthing, Norfolk. This does not belong to the helmet (No. 34) found at the same place. The figure of Mars and the head of Medusa can be seen in the photograph; the left cheek is ornamented with a figure of Victory. Height 8 in. Norwich Castle Museum.

36 Great Dish from the Late Roman hoard of silver table-ware, Mildenhall, Suffolk. The outer frieze on this early fourth-century dish of Mediterranean origin represents the triumph of Bacchus over Hercules. The central medallion depicts the head of a sea-god, probably Oceanus. Diameter $23\frac{3}{4}$ in. British Museum.

37 Bronze statuette of the Emperor Nero. Often ascribed to Barking Hall, Suffolk, but almost certainly from a rural shrine at Coddenham, Suffolk. Height 19½ in. British Museum.

38 Jet plaque bearing human figure wearing Phrygian cap, possibly associated with Mithraic worship, from Roman villa at Whitton, Ipswich, Suffolk. Height of fragment 2½ in. Ipswich Museum.

39 Bezel of fourth-century Roman gold ring, Brancaster, Norfolk. The Latin inscription VIVAS IN DEO indicates its Christian origin. Width of bezel about ⅓ in. Norwich Castle Museum.

40 Pair of Roman iron shackles from the River Wensum at Worthing, Norfolk. (Same site as Nos. 34 and 35, but not associated.) The barrel-padlock securing these shackles, presumably for a slave or prisoner, has been forced. Length of padlock about 5½ in. Norwich Castle Museum.

41 Bronze ceremonial head-dress, Hockwold-cum-Wilton, Norfolk. This late fourth-century head-dress was one of six found at a probable temple site, and doubtless formed part of the priestly regalia. Maximum height 5¾ in. British Museum. Replicas in Bury Museum and Norwich Castle Museum.

42 Bronze ceremonial head-dress, Hockwold-cum-Wilton, Norfolk. This head-dress, part of the hoard mentioned above, was formerly decorated with three silver plaques, of which only one remains, and has an adjustable head-band. Maximum height 2⅞ in. British Museum. Replicas in Bury Museum and Norwich Castle Museum.

43 Runic inscription on sheep's astragalus from the Anglo-Saxon cemetery at Caistor-by-Norwich, Norfolk. This was found with a cremation in a fifth-century urn and doubtless served some magical purpose as the inscription seems intentionally obscure. Maximum length 1 1/16 in. Norwich Castle Museum.

44 Ogham inscription on knife-handle of red deer antler, Weeting, Norfolk. This inscription, which dates from the sixth to eighth centuries, is cut

on both sides of the handle. Similar inscriptions on portable objects have been found in the Pictish culture of north Scotland, but none has been satisfactorily translated. Length 2¾ in. Norwich Castle Museum.

45 The stone sceptre from the Sutton Hoo ship-burial, Suffolk. This remarkable ceremonial object, doubtless part of the insignia of the East Anglian royal family, is in the form of a whetstone with decorated terminals. A gloomy human mask appears on each face at one end. Length 22½ in. British Museum.

46 Gold pendant of seventh-century Kentish work found on the foreshore between Bacton and Mundesley, Norfolk. This consists of a gold coin of the Emperor Mauricius, minted about 600, once set around with garnets separated by gold foil. Diameter 1⅜ in. British Museum.

47 Purse-lid from ship-burial, Sutton Hoo, Suffolk. The purse, which contained 40 Merovingian gold coins, has perished leaving only this magnificent gold frame set with garnets and mosaic glass. The internal mounts include two of a human figure between two animals, two more of falcons swooping on ducks, and two hexagonal mounts of intricate design in which small garnets are set in gold 'mushroom cells', a technique characteristic of the Sutton Hoo jewellery. Length 7½ in. British Museum.

48 After-part of ship in barrow, Sutton Hoo, Suffolk, during excavation in 1939. None of the wood of the vessel had survived, the apparent ribs being of consolidated sand; the iron clench nails revealed the lines of the ship. This was a clinker-built, rowing vessel, 86 feet long, with a cabin amidships containing the treasure.

49 Iron visored helmet from the ship-burial at Sutton Hoo, Suffolk. This ceremonial helmet of sixth-century Swedish workmanship is lavishly ornamented with gilt-bronze, silver wire, niello, gold foil and garnets. The helmet is covered with rectangular panels, some embossed with figures and others with interlace ornament. Circumference above brow 26½ in. British Museum.

50 Part of the seventh–ninth century inhumation cemetery, Caister-by-Yarmouth, Norfolk, during excavation in 1954. This area of the cemetery lay outside the ditches of the Roman town, adjacent to the road leading to the harbour. The orientation and general lack of grave-goods suggest that these are Christian burials, but the presence of about a dozen 'pseudo-ship-burials' indicates a survival of pagan tradition.

51 Late Saxon pottery kiln, Thetford, Norfolk, looking into stokehole, during excavation in 1949. This kiln and others near by produced Thetford ware in the early eleventh century; when discovered this kiln contained cooking-pots and lamps from the last firing.

52 Viking stirrup of ninth–tenth century date, dredged from river Thet, Kilverstone, Norfolk. This iron stirrup is inlaid with brass, some forming a running spiral pattern. Height $9\frac{1}{4}$ in. Norwich Castle Museum.

53 Hilt of Viking sword of tenth–eleventh century date, Mileham, Norfolk. The pommel and guard are of brass and the blade is pattern-welded. It was found close to the site of the drawbridge of a Medieval moated homestead. Length of sword 2 ft $9\frac{1}{2}$ in., length of hilt $6\frac{1}{8}$ in. Norwich Castle Museum.

54 Stone cross from St Vedast church, Norwich. This weathered sandstone cross bears panels with zoomorphic decoration and interlace, showing strong Scandinavian influence, and dates from the tenth century. The survey mark at the top is modern. Height 3 ft. Norwich Castle Museum.

55 Head of stone cross in Whissonsett church, Norfolk. This is part of a wheel-head cross of East Anglian type of late tenth–early eleventh century date. It is carved on all four faces with interlace. Height of surviving fragment 2 ft 5 in.

56 Late Saxon cathedral, North Elmham, Norfolk. On the left is the base of the turret staircase of the early eleventh-century west tower, built of local ferruginous conglomerate. The flanking tower on the right is an addition of the late fourteenth century, when the cathedral was converted into a manor-house by Henry Despencer, Bishop of Norwich.

57 Air view of Norman castle, Castle Rising, Norfolk, looking east. The stone keep was built about the middle of the twelfth century by William d'Albini, but the earthworks are earlier. The central ring-motte is flanked on the east and west by rectangular enclosures; its ditch has been deepened and the enlarged rampart now partly covers the remains of an apsidal twelfth-century chapel.

58 Air view of motte-and-bailey castle, Horsford, Norfolk, looking west. On the right are the remains of the motte, separated from its horseshoe-shaped bailey by a ditch which was spanned by a bridge. This latter was protected at its outer end by a barbican. The original eleventh-century Norman castle of earth and timber was modified at a later date when a stone keep was constructed on the motte.

59 Air view of Cluniac priory, Castle Acre, Norfolk, looking north. Most of the buildings of this priory, founded 1089, are of twelfth-century date. The church lies on the north side of the monastery, with the square cloister on its south. The domestic buildings and frater lie west and south of the cloister, while to its east are the chapter house, dorter and infirmary; the rere dorter lies at the south end of these buildings.

60 Air view of Barton Broad, Norfolk, looking north. The islands are the remains of baulks between Medieval peat-pits, and their direction changes at the old parish boundary. The artificial origin of this broad was suggested by Samuel Woodward as long ago as 1834, and has been proven for this and other broads by intensive boring and documentary research during recent years.

Index

Date Due

NO 2'81			
	PRINTED	IN U. S. A.	